Russian Case Morpholog

Linguistic Inquiry Monographs

Samuel Jay Keyser, general editor

Russian Case Morphology and the Syntactic Categories

David Pesetsky

The MIT Press
Cambridge, Massachusetts
London, England

MIT Press books may be purchased at special quantity discounts for business or sales promotional use. For information, please email special_sales@mitpress.mit.edu.

This book was set in Syntax and Times by Toppan Best-set Premedia Limited. Printed and bound in the United States of America.

Library of Congress Cataloging-in-Publication Data
Pesetsky, David Michael.
Russian case morphology and the syntactic categories / David Pesetsky.
pages cm. — (Linguistic inquiry monographs)
Includes bibliographical references and index.
ISBN 978-0-262-01972-9 (hardcover : alk. paper) 1. Russian language–Case.
2. Russian language—Morphology. 3. Russian language—Syntax. 4. Grammar,
Comparative and general—Nominals. I. Title.
PG2221.P47 2013
491.75—dc23
2013011184

10 9 8 7 6 5 4 3 2 1

To Morris Halle,
who taught me that Russian is always more complicated than I think it is,
but less complicated than it looks

Contents

Series Foreword

We are pleased to present the sixty-sixth volume in the series *Linguistic Inquiry Monographs*. These monographs present new and original research beyond the scope of the article. We hope they will benefit our field by bringing to it perspectives that will stimulate further research and insight.

Originally published in limited edition, the *Linguistic Inquiry Monographs* are now more widely available. This change is due to the great interest engendered by the series and by the needs of a growing readership. The editors thank the readers for their support and welcome suggestions about future directions for the series.

Samuel Jay Keyser
for the Editorial Board

Acknowledgments

This work owes its existence to two events in 2007. The first was a paper by my colleague Norvin Richards (2007; published as Richards 2013). Norvin's paper analyzed the interaction between the lexical/structural case distinction and case stacking in the Australian language Lardil, and advanced the insane hypothesis that Russian might actually be a "case-stacking language" just like Lardil—despite the (superficial) absence of anything like case stacking in Russian.

The second event was an invitation to speak at the 16th Formal Approaches to Slavic Linguistics (FASL) conference at Stony Brook University in May 2007. At the time, I had not worked intensively on Russian for almost a quarter century. It was this invitation that sent me back to this wonderful language once again (admittedly somewhat panicked), in search of unsolved problems that might prove both tractable and paper-worthy. One of the most notorious unsolved problems of Russian is the syntax of numerals, and to this day I do not have a clear idea why I chose to return to Russian syntax by such an unpromising path. As it turned out, however, I had a tool in hand that previous researchers had lacked, which offered a new perspective on the puzzle: Norvin's conjecture that Russian might be a case-stacking language "under the hood."

In the end, a very rough proposal about the Russian numerals was presented at the conference—a proposal that, after many years of off-and-on research on the project, developed into the work reported here. I am deeply grateful to Norvin for providing one of the key ideas of this monograph, to the organizers of FASL for the invitation that compelled me to start the project in the first place, and to many students and other colleagues who have shared their questions, comments, and objections.

For particularly valuable discussion, I am especially grateful to John Bailyn, Danny Fox, Ora Matushansky, Maria Polinsky, Norvin Richards, Erich Schoorlemmer, Sergei Tatevosov, Esther Torrego, and Coppe van Urk, and to students at the 2007 New York–St. Petersburg Institute, a spring 2009 seminar on case at MIT, the 2009 EGG summer school in Poznań, the 2009 EALING fall school in Paris, the 2010 LOT summer school in Nijmegen, and the 2012 LISSIM summer school in India. I also want to thank the Cambridge community of Russophone linguists (Alya Asarina, Natalia Ivlieva, Liudmila Nikolaeva, Alexander Podobryaev, Maria Polinsky, Kirill Shklovsky, and Igor Yanovich) for discussion of everything from theory to judgments—and particularly special thanks go to Natalia Ivlieva, for comments and Russian-language assistance on the very first draft of this monograph.

For smart, constructive comments on earlier versions of this monograph (in some cases, extremely detailed), I am grateful to Željko Bošković, Greville Corbett, Pavel Caha, Ora Matushansky, Irina Mikaelian, Asya Pereltsvaig, Yakov Testelets, Bartosz Wiland, Michael Yadroff, and four anonymous reviewers for MIT Press.

Finally, special thanks to Anne Mark for superb copyediting of the manuscript (even spotting typos in Russian examples).

Единственное число при таких словах, как *два*, *три* и *четыре*, где ясно указана множественность, представляется на первый взгляд очень странным и является характерным примером того, насколько грамматическое мышление может расходиться с логическим.

The singular with such words as *dva* 'two', *tri* 'three', and *četyre* 'four', where plurality is clearly indicated, seems at first glance very strange, and constitutes a typical example of the extent to which grammatical and logical thinking may diverge.

Aleksandr Peškovskij, *Russkij sintaksis v naučnom osveščenii*[1]

1 Introduction to the Puzzles

It is the oddest facts that sometimes provide the most useful clues to significant properties of language. In this monograph, I argue that the peculiarities of Russian nominal phrases provide clues of just this sort concerning the syntactic side of morphological case. In fact, the richest evidence will come from the most peculiar of these phrases: those that involve a member of the closed class traditionally called the *paucal numerals*. This class includes the low numerals *dva* 'two', *oba* 'both', *tri* 'three', and *četyre* 'four', as well as several expressions of fractional quantity that I will not discuss at any length (*pol* 'half', *poltora* 'one and a half', and certain uses of *četvert'* 'quarter'; Mel'čuk 1985, 322ff.). I will call these elements "paucals" rather than "paucal numerals," for reasons that will become clear in chapter 4.

The peculiar behavior of nominal phrases with paucals can be easily observed by constructing minimal pairs like (1a–b), which differ only in the presence versus absence of a paucal. Both examples exhibit the forms found in nominative environments, such as subject of a finite clause.

(1) a. **No paucal (or nonpaucal numeral) (nominative environment)**
No mismatches

èt-**i**	posledn-**ie**	krasiv-**ye**	stol-**y**
these-**NOM.PL**	last-**NOM.PL**	beautiful-**NOM.PL**	table-**NOM.PL**

'these last beautiful tables'

b. **With paucal (nominative environment)**
Case mismatch, number mismatch

èt-**i**	posledn-**ie**	dv-**a**	krasiv-**yx**
these-**NOM.PL**	last-**NOM.PL**	two-**M.NOM**	beautiful-*GEN*.**PL**

stol-**a**
table-*GEN.SG*

'these last two beautiful tables'

In (1a), the demonstrative, adjectives, and noun agree in both number (plural) and case (nominative), just as one expects from a well-behaved Indo-European language. When a paucal such as *dva* 'two' is added, however, as in (1b), two types of mismatch appear:

• **Number mismatch:** The noun is *singular*; but the modifiers and demonstrative are *plural*.

• **Case mismatch:** The noun and adjective that follow the paucal show *genitive* case; but the paucal, along with the demonstrative and adjective that precede it, are *nominative*.[1]

Complicating the picture further, if the paucal in (1b) is replaced with a nonpaucal numeral such as *pjat'* 'five', the case mismatch remains, but the number mismatch disappears.[2] The noun is now plural, as seen in (2).

(2) **With nonpaucal numeral (nominative environment)**
    Case mismatch, but no number mismatch
    èt-**i**   posledn-**ie**   pjat'   krasiv-**yx**
    these-**NOM.PL** last-**NOM.PL** five.**NOM** beautiful-**GEN.PL**
    stol-**ov**
    table-**GEN.***PL*
    'these last five beautiful tables'

Finally, in oblique-case environments (exemplified here by the dative), all mismatches disappear, regardless of the presence or absence of paucals and nonpaucal numerals. Instead, we find what Babby (1987, 100) calls the "homogeneous pattern," as opposed to the "heterogeneous" patterns of (1b) and (2): full agreement in case and number.[3]

(3) a. **No paucal (or nonpaucal numeral) (oblique environment)**
       No mismatches
       èt-**im**   posledn-**im**   krasiv-**ym**   stol-**am**
       these-**DAT.PL**   last-**DAT.PL**   beautiful-**DAT.PL**   table-**DAT.PL**
       'these last beautiful tables'
    b. **With paucal (oblique environment)**
       No mismatches
       èt-**im**   posledn-**im**   dvu-**m**   krasiv-**ym**
       these-**DAT.PL**   last-**DAT.PL**   two-**DAT.PL**   beautiful-**DAT.PL**
       stol-**am**
       table-**DAT.PL**
       'to these last two beautiful tables'

c. **With nonpaucal numeral (oblique environment)**
No mismatches

èt-**im**	posledn-**im**	pjat-**i**	krasiv-**ym**
these-**DAT.PL**	last-**DAT.PL**	five-**DAT**	beautiful-**DAT.PL**

stol-**am**

table-**DAT.PL**

'to these last five beautiful tables'

On the face of it, the facts collected in (1)–(3) may look like mere eccentricities of the language. In keeping with the dictum with which this monograph began, however, I will argue that they are not eccentricities at all, but predictable patterns whose explanation sheds light on the very nature of case morphology and the laws that govern its distribution.

2   Do We Need the Traditional Case Categories?

It is an obvious fact about Russian that most nouns, adjectives, numerals, and demonstratives bear a case suffix, and that the choice of case suffix is determined by two factors: *morphological environment* (the lexical properties of the stem to which the suffix attaches) and *syntactic environment*. The traditional cross-classification of Russian case affixes by case category ("nominative," "genitive," etc.) versus declension class and gender directly reflects the distinct roles of syntactic and morphological environment in determining the choice of case suffix.[1] At the same time, though the traditional case categories do reflect the syntactic side of morphological case, it is a striking fact that they are irrelevant elsewhere in syntax. They are sui generis categories relevant only to the theory of case itself. This observation is not merely terminological, but reflects a substantive claim: that case morphology, though governed by rules that refer to the syntax, constitutes an *independent level of linguistic analysis*, whose function is to mediate between the categories and configurations of syntax and the actual forms supplied by the morphology.

This should not strike us as a comfortable conclusion. All things being equal, one hopes that independent mediating levels of this sort will turn out to be eliminable from the theory of grammar. Otherwise, they raise but leave unanswered the question: why are they there? In a better world, the apparent need for special case terminology would turn out to reflect a mere inadequacy of understanding rather than an actual property of human languages. Unfortunately, however, we do not yet live in that better world. To the best of my knowledge, no characterization of languages like Russian has managed to dispense with some version of the traditional roster of cases—for good reasons.

Suppose, for example, one were to attempt a theory of the syntactic distribution of the Russian case suffixes in which all reference to a case category like "genitive" is eliminated in favor of direct reference to the actual suffixes (-*a*, -*y*, etc.). Such a proposal would leave unexplained the fact that the *syntactic* generalizations relevant to the choice of suffix are utterly insensitive to their phonological shape. A syntactic environment that calls for genitive case never cares that it might be realized in many ways (depending on the declension class, gender, number, and syntactic category of the stem): as -a, -y, -ov, -ej, -ogo, -oj, -yx, or a surface zero. There are syntactic environments that require or disallow genitive case, but no syntactic environment that requires or disallows, for example, the suffix -a or -y. Similar observations can be made for all the case categories of Russian. From this, we conclude that reference to notions like "genitive" cannot be eliminated in favor of reference to actual suffixes such as -a or -y.

Suppose instead that one were to attempt the other obvious reduction: eliminating the special case categories in favor of direct reference to categories and configurations independently motivated within syntax. This enterprise too might seem doomed from the outset—if only because, at least at first glance, the mapping between Russian case and sentence-level syntax looks complex and decidedly not one-to-one. If we were to restrict our attention to examples like (1a) and (2), for example, it could be imagined that the term "genitive" is eliminable in favor of the purely syntactic notion "postpaucal/postnumeral." In fact, however, as we saw in (3b–c), postnumeral position sometimes fails to trigger genitive morphology. Furthermore, sets of suffixes identical to those found in postnumeral position in (1b) and (2) also appear in other syntactic configurations (as possessors and complements of N, for example).[2]

It is probably for reasons like these that researchers have consistently posited the existence of case-specific notions such as "genitive" as an essential ingredient of the interface between syntax and morphology. It has generally seemed an inescapable conclusion that the rules of syntax assign words and phrases to case categories, and the rules of morphology determine how case categories are realized—with the case categories themselves functioning as a *middleman*, mediating between syntactic configuration and morphological realization.[3]

It seems to me, however, that though the arguments against replacing the list of case categories with lists of actual suffixes are straightforward, the arguments against a *reduction to syntax* are considerably less compelling—if only because our understanding of the syntactic side of case remains so strikingly incomplete. Because the distribution of case forms across syntactic configurations still presents numerous complex and unsolved puzzles, it is at least conceivable that the solution to one or more open questions about the syntax of case might allow us to "eliminate the middleman" after all, by reducing the case categories to independently attested properties of the syntax.

The goal of this monograph is to suggest a possible advance of just this sort. The starting point will be an account for the pattern of case and number mismatches shown in (1)–(3). I will argue on the basis of an analysis of the special properties of constructions with paucals and nonpaucal numerals that the Russian cases are not independent categories, but are actually affixal realizations of the various *parts of speech*, as shown in (4).

(4) **Reduction of the Russian cases to part-of-speech categories**

Genitive	= N	Accusative	= V
Nominative	= D	Obliques	= P

If this proposal is correct, a genitive-marked word is simply a stem to which a morpheme of category N has been attached; a nominative-marked word is a stem with an affix of category D; an accusative-marked word bears an affix of category V; and an oblique-marked (dative, instrumental, prepositional, or locative) word bears an affix of category P.[4] Only the distinctions among these oblique cases in Russian will fail to correspond to a traditional part-of-speech distinction. My hope is that the differences among dative, instrumental, prepositional, and locative cases will turn out to reflect the properties that independently distinguish subcategories of overt prepositions, but I will not make an explicit proposal to this effect—so this aspect of the proposal will remain incomplete. Genitive case is, of course, traditionally grouped with the oblique cases, but it is treated separately here, for reasons that will become clear in the next chapter.

Throughout the monograph, when discussing the various cases in the context of the proposal summarized in (4), I will often use the abbreviations N_{GEN}, D_{NOM}, V_{ACC}, and P_{OBL} (or P_{DAT}, etc.) to remind us of the traditional names for the cases whose actual nature is simply N, D, V, and P (or P with additional features).[5]

At the heart of the analysis will be an account of how N_{GEN}, D_{NOM}, V_{ACC}, and P_{DAT} end up as case suffixes on nouns, adjectives, demonstratives, paucals, and nonpaucal numerals. I will argue that there are two paths by which part-of-speech suffixes end up on words.

One path by which a part-of-speech suffix may end up on a word is by *assignment in the course of the syntactic derivation*, a process in which part-of-speech features of an *assigner* (along with certain other grammatical features) are copied onto one or more *recipients*. The notion that case has an assigner and an assignee recalls many older proposals that also posited rules of case assignment under particular structural conditions (Vergnaud 2006 [orig. 1976]; Chomsky 1980, 1981; Rouveret and Vergnaud 1980)—and strongly recalls Emonds's (1987, 615) principle of *Alternative Realization*, a generalization of case assignment to all instances of inflection, as Bartosz Wiland (personal communication) has pointed out.

(5) **Feature Assignment (FA), version 1 of 6**[6]

    a. *Copying:* When α merges with β, forming $[_\alpha\ \alpha\ \beta]$, the grammatical features of α are immediately copied onto β, …

    b. *Realization:* … and are realized as morphology on all lexical items dominated by β.

Two independent properties of syntax will interact with the FA rule (5) in particularly illuminating ways. One is *movement*, which, by altering the structural relation between α and β, may block feature copying (case assignment) from α to β. The other is the rule of *Spell-Out* that has been argued to apply whenever a particular type of syntactic domain called a *phase* is created (Chomsky 2001, 2004). Spell-Out establishes and fixes the pronunciation of the terminal elements of a phase, and sends this information from the syntax to the phonology, where it may not be altered by any subsequent operation of the syntax, including FA. The value of these two processes (movement and Spell-Out) for our discussion will lie in their ability to freeze for our inspection earlier stages of the derivation that might otherwise reflect the morphological consequences of feature copying. This will allow us to test predictions concerning that derivation, and will play a crucial role in the account of (1)–(3).

The second path by which a part-of-speech suffix may end up on a word is *lexical*. If (4) is correct, every element that comes from the lexicon as a noun, determiner, verb, or preposition could equally well be described as coming from the lexicon assigned to the corresponding case categories. In other words, from the point of view of the syntax, every noun can be described as "born genitive," every verb as "born accusative," every determiner as "born nominative," and every preposition as "born oblique."

For uninflected, monomorphemic words, it is hard to find empirical predictions that can test such proposals—for example, that a dative-assigning preposition like Russian *k* 'to' assigns PDAT to its complement because the preposition itself belongs to the category PDAT.[7] The possible consequences of FA are much more obvious, however, for inflected categories such as nouns. If Marantz (1997) and others are correct in suggesting that the core of every noun is a category-neutral root to which a categorizing morpheme is added (as head of the newly formed word), a noun to which no other case has been assigned will always take the form **[[root] NGEN]**; that is, it will bear what traditional descriptions call genitive case.[8] This means that the presence of NGEN morphology on a noun does not necessarily reflect the result of the rule FA in (5), but might represent the noun's "primeval" state—that is, the form in which it entered the syntactic derivation, as in (6).[9]

(6) **"Primeval genitive" conjecture**

NGEN categorizes a Russian root as a noun (in the lexicon).

We also expect, however, to find other instances of NGEN morphology that *are* assigned. For example, if FA is a correct proposal, because a noun *is* a word of category NGEN, it will also assign NGEN to anything that merges with it. And indeed, most Russian nouns do assign genitive to adnominals, a fact that will provide converging evidence in section 4.2 for the idea that nouns are "born genitive."[10]

If nouns are "born genitive," of course, immediate questions arise concerning the morphology of all those nouns that do not *look* genitive—for example, nouns whose sole visible case suffix realizes DNOM or VACC, or one of the POBL cases. This is the principal topic of the next chapter, in which I begin to develop the account of (1)–(3).

3 Russian as a Case-Stacking Language

3.1 The One-Suffix Rule in Russian

The "primeval genitive" conjecture in (6) is a clear nonstarter, unless we can explain why NGEN morphology is not visible whenever the noun bears any other kind of case morphology. On the proposal sketched in chapter 2, a nominative-marked noun should be the result of merging D to an NP whose head bears primeval NGEN—followed by copying of DNOM morphology onto the terminals of that NP, in accordance with (5). In fact, however, the surface form of nominative nouns in Russian shows no evidence of an NGEN suffix inside the DNOM. Thus, either (4), (5), and (6) are false, or else DNOM morphology must somehow *suppress* the pronunciation of the NGEN morphology with which the noun entered the syntax. Fortunately for (6), this is not a property particular to DNOM and NGEN. It is a pervasive fact about Russian that no noun, adjective, or determiner bears more than one visible case suffix.[1] The grammar of Russian must therefore include some rule with the effect of (7), independent of the truth of (6).

(7) **The One-Suffix Rule (later replaced by (125))**
   Delete all but the outermost case suffix.

Let us see how the One-Suffix Rule works in tandem with (4), (5), and (6).[2] Since the shape of case morphology is sensitive to morphological environment, we must first be careful to distinguish the affixation of NGEN, a syntactic feature-bundle, from the *realization* of these features as actual suffixes. The examples in (8) show the varying shape of NGEN morphology for regular nouns of declension classes 1 and 2.

(8) **Realization of NGEN on singular and plural nouns**

	Stem	NGEN sg.		Stem	NGEN pl.		
a.	stol	-a	b.	stol	-ov	'table'	(class 1)
c.	lamp	-y	d.	lamp	-ъ	'lamp'	(class 2)

I use the Cyrillic character ъ in (8d) and elsewhere to indicate a suffix that is phonologically zero on the surface. In some analyses of Russian phonology, this suffix is an underlying vowel called a "yer" (historically a lax high vowel), realized as zero in (8d), but capable of surfacing as a full vowel elsewhere (Lightner 1972). The precise phonology of the suffix is not important to this monograph,[3] but its reality as a morpheme is. For one thing, if the discussion in the previous chapter is correct, then without the affixation of NGEN, the root *lamp-* 'lamp' would not be categorized as N and usable as a noun in the syntax. Furthermore, as we will see shortly, superficially zero case morphemes are visible to the One-Suffix Rule.[4]

Suppose, as I have claimed, that nominative morphology on the terminal elements of an NP arises as a consequence of FA. When NP merges with DNOM (forming a DP), the part-of-speech features of DNOM are copied onto the NP and realized on the lexical items that NP dominates. Were it not for the One-Suffix Rule, the expected result might be visible *case stacking* on the noun— that is, pronunciation of both an NGEN suffix and a DNOM suffix. The One-Suffix Rule, however, guarantees that such case stacking will not be observable in surface forms. The examples in (9) show the posited underlying stacking of DNOM outside NGEN, as well as the consequence of the One-Suffix Rule for the surface appearance of the nominative forms of the lexical items in (8) (indicated by parentheses surrounding suppressed suffixes).

(9) **Suppression of NGEN by DNOM (indicated by parentheses)**

	Stem	NGEN sg.	DNOM sg.		Stem	NGEN pl.	DNOM pl.	
a.	stol	(-a)	-ъ	b.	stol	(-ov)	-y	'table'
	by (7): **stol**				by (7): **stoly**			
c.	lamp	(-y)	-a	d.	lamp	(-ъ)	-y	'lamp'
	by (7): **lampa**				by (7): **lampy**			

Note that the phonologically null suffix -ъ in (9a) suppresses the (otherwise nonnull) genitive -*a*, an argument in favor of the existence of the -ъ suffix, if the overall proposal is correct.

Let us now consider the consequences of merging an oblique-assigning P with a DP. Crucially, I will assume throughout this monograph that oblique case is *always* the result of morphology assigned by P. When oblique morphology is found on the object of an overt preposition (such as dative-assigning *k* 'to' or instrumental-assigning *pod* 'under'), I will argue that the overt preposition assigns the case. When there is no overt preposition, I will assume that there is a null preposition—as argued independently for languages such as Basque by Rezac (2008), among others. When a preposition (overt or null) merges with DP, the POBL morphology assigned by P to the lexical items of DP should suppress the pronunciation of DNOM suffixes, just as DNOM suppressed NGEN. (Throughout this monograph, I exemplify POBL with dative.) The facts once more accord with the One-Suffix Rule.

(10) **Suppression of DNOM morphology by POBL (PDAT)**

	Stem	NGEN sg.	DNOM sg.	PDAT sg.		Stem	NGEN pl.	DNOM pl.	PDAT sg.
a.	**stol**	(-a)	(-ъ)	**-u**	b.	**stol**	(-ov)	(-y)	**-am**
	by (7): *stolu*					by (7): *stolam*			
c.	**lamp**	(-y)	(-a)	**-e**	d.	**lamp**	(-ъ)	(-y)	**-am**
	by (7): *lampe*					by (7): *lampam*			

A proposal with the goals outlined in chapters 1 and 2 is thus driven to the conclusion that Russian is a case-stacking language "behind the scenes," with the One-Suffix Rule responsible for the fact that overt case stacking is not visible in Russian.

3.2 Case Stacking in Lardil

We might, of course, worry (even at this preliminary stage) about the inherent plausibility of the very idea that a language might allow case stacking whose effects are hidden by a case-morpheme deletion rule. Languages with *overt* case stacking, though uncommon, do exist. One well-known example is Lardil, a highly endangered Tangkic language of northern Australia, whose patterns of case stacking were first investigated in depth by Ken Hale. Lardil case stacking has been discussed by Klokeid (1976), by Hale (1997, 1998), and most recently by Richards (2007, 2013), whose analysis of the phenomenon inspired many aspects of the present monograph. (I am also grateful to Norvin Richards for his assistance with the Lardil sections of this monograph.) Lardil provides some of the initial reassurance we need—not only that case stacking exists, but also that its effects may be hidden by a deletion operation like the One-Suffix Rule in languages besides Russian.

Lardil is a nominative-accusative language. Case morphology assigned to a nominal phrase (which I will assume is an instance of DP) is normally observed on every dependent of the nominal. Example (11) shows ACC morphology on the demonstrative, adjective, and noun of an object DP.

(11) **VACC on all terminal elements within DP (Lardil)**

Kara	nyingki	kurri	[kiin-i	mutha-n	thungal-i]?
Q	you	see	that-ACC	big-ACC	tree-ACC

'Do you see that big tree?'
(Richards 2007; 2013, 46 ex. (12))

As Hale (1998, 198) notes, "[T]his behavior is altogether familiar, from Latin, German or Russian, for example," as we have already seen in Russian examples like the NOM (1a) and DAT (3). The distribution of ACC in the Russian example (12) is directly comparable to that in the Lardil example (11).

(12) **VACC on all terminal elements within DP (Russian)**

Ty	vidiš'	t-u	bol'š-uju	ëlk-u?
you.NOM	see	that-F.ACC.SG	big-F.ACC.SG	fir.tree-ACC.SG

'Do you see that big fir tree?'

On the view advanced in this monograph, we would propose that V in both (11) and (12) has assigned its complement DP VACC morphology, which has then been realized as morphology on the terminal elements of the DP, following the rule FA in (5). I return to the gender and number properties of the Russian examples below, and I discuss Russian accusative in more detail in chapter 7.

In a similar vein, we would propose that N assigns NGEN morphology to a possessor DP in sentences like (13) and its Russian counterparts (to which I return in chapters 8 and 9).

(13) **NGEN on possessor DP (Lardil)**

[Ngithun	yaku]	wirima-kun	nguku-n.
I.GEN	sister.NOM	bring-ACTUAL	water-ACC

'My sister brought some water.'
(Klokeid 1976, 206 ex. (4d))

The possessed DP in (13) is assigned NOM, whose case morphology is null in Lardil. Famously, however, when a GEN possessor is contained within a DP assigned a case whose morphology is *not* null, we see overt and obvious case stacking. The case morphology assigned to the possessee DP is also assigned to its possessor and appears as a second case suffix following the GEN suffix that was assigned to the possessor by the possessee N. The examples in (14) illustrate this. Example (14a) shows the stacking of ACC morphology outside GEN on the possessor in a direct object DP, while example (14b) shows case stacking in a DP marked with instrumental (INSTR) case; here, INSTR morphology appears outside GEN on the possessor.

(14) **ACC, INSTR stacking outside GEN (Lardil)**

a. *GEN-ACC stacking*

Ngada	derlde	marun-ngan-i	wangalk-i.
I	break	boy-GEN-ACC	boomerang-ACC

'I broke the boy's boomerang.'
(Richards 2007; 2013, 49 ex. (20a))

b. *GEN-INSTR stacking*

Ngada	latha	karnjin-i	[marun-ngan-ku	maarn-ku].
I	spear	wallaby-ACC	boy-GEN-INSTR	spear-INSTR

'I speared the wallaby with the boy's spear.'
(Richards 2007; 2013, 43 ex. (3))

As Richards notes, the order of the stacked case suffixes mirrors the order in which the heads responsible for these suffixes merge as the clause is built: first, GEN morphology is added when the possessor DP merges with N, and only later is ACC or INSTR added (when ACC-assigning V or a null INSTR-assigning P is merged).

Since Lardil shows case stacking overtly, either it must lack the One-Suffix Rule that prevents overt case stacking in the current proposal for Russian, or else the GEN morphology assigned to possessors must be some kind of exception to the rule. In fact, the One-Suffix Rule does appear to be active elsewhere in Lardil, suggesting that the case stacking seen in (14) is indeed a Lardil-specific exception to a general case-deletion process that Lardil otherwise shares with Russian.

In Lardil, as in some other Australian languages, tense morphology may be assigned to nominals. In this monograph, I follow my sources in focusing on future morphology assigned in this manner, but nonfuture morphology also participates in this process. (Richards (2013, 47 n. 3) notes that the suffix usually called "future" is probably a more general irrealis marker, but I follow him in maintaining the label "future.") Example (15) shows the future (FUT) suffix attached not only to the main verb, but also to the direct object.

(15) **FUT morphology on V and direct object DP (Lardil)**

Ngada	warnawu-**thur**	yak-**ur**.
I.NOM	cook-**FUT**	fish-**FUT**

'I will cook the fish.'
(Richards 2007; 2013, 48 ex. (17a))

This FUT marking, like ACC in examples like (12), is found on every dependent of the direct object of a FUT-marked verb, and on INSTR-marked phrases as well, as seen in example (16b). Example (16a) shows a nonfuture version of the crucial example, for comparison. Note that this example also shows stacking of FUT outside INSTR.

(16) FUT **morphology on all terminal elements in vP (Lardil)**

    a. *Baseline: Nonfuture*

        Ngada   nguthungu   warnawu   dulnhuka-n   beerr-u

        I   slowly   cook   month.fish-ACC   ti.tree-INSTR

        nyith-u.

        fire-INSTR

        'I slowly cooked the month fish on a fire of ti-tree wood.'

    b. *Future*

        Ngada   nguthunguthu-r   warnawu-thur   dulnhuka-r

        I   slowly-FUT   cook-FUT   month.fish-FUT

        beerr-uru-r   nyith-uru-r.

        ti.tree-INSTR-FUT   fire-INSTR-FUT

        'I will slowly cook the month fish on a fire of ti-tree wood.'

        (Richards 2007; 2013, 48 exx. (16a–b))

FUT marking also appears stacked outside GEN on a possessor, as (17) shows.

(17) GEN-FUT **stacking**

        Ngada   derlde-thu   marun-ngan-ku   wangalk-u.

        I   break-FUT   boy-GEN-FUT   boomerang-FUT

        'I will break the boy's boomerang.'

        (Richards 2007; 2013, 49 ex. (20b))

I propose that the FUT morphology is assigned by T (i.e., that it is TFUT). FA assigns TFUT to the vP sister of T, so future morphology ends up on the terminal elements of vP by the same process operative in (12). As predicted if FUT morphology is assigned by T to the terminal elements of its sister vP, the subject is not marked with FUT.[5]

As Richards notes, an important question now arises. Since Lardil is a language with overt case stacking, why is FUT on the direct object not stacked outside an ACC suffix? If V assigns ACC, and T is merged later than V, we expect to see FUT stacked outside ACC in a language with overt case stacking—but no ACC is observed in such configurations. I propose that ACC has been deleted as a consequence of the One-Suffix Rule. Though possessor GEN in (14) and INSTR in (16b) are exceptions to the rule, ACC is not.

The correctness of this hypothesis, of course, is not self-evident. One might hypothesize alternatively that FUT marking is actually a flavor of accusative—that is, a case assigned by V instead of the usual ACC, whenever V is future-marked. On this hypothesis, we do not need to attribute the absence of normal ACC marking to the One-Suffix Rule or any other deletion process. Nonfuture ACC was simply never assigned in the first place. Richards provides a compelling argument against this view (building on an observation by Hale (1997, 44)) and in favor of the view that ACC is indeed assigned to FUT-marked direct objects like the direct object in (16b) and subsequently deleted. He observes first that relative clauses are not barriers to the assignment of case morphology. As (18) shows, ACC morphology assigned to a direct object modified by a relative clause spreads to the members of the relative clause as well.

(18) **VACC assigned to a direct object extends into relative clause as well (Lardil)**

Kara	nyingki	kurri	kiin-i	mutha-n	thungal-i,
Q	you	see	that-ACC	big-ACC	tree-ACC

[ngithun-i   kirdi-thuru-Ø]?
I.GEN-ACC   cut-FUT-ACC[6]
'Do you see that big tree, which I am going to cut down?'
(Richards 2007; 2013, 52 ex. (29a))

Note also that the first-person subject of the relative clause in (18) is marked GEN (with stacked ACC), a phenomenon reminiscent of *ga-no* conversion in Japanese (as Richards remarks) and comparable phenomena in the Turkic languages. We might tentatively view this as morphology assigned by the higher N, which appears inside stacked VACC—just as FA predicts, given the transparency of Lardil relative clauses and the order of derivation.

Remarkably, when FUT morphology appears on a direct object, the members of the relative clause are marked, not with FUT, but with ACC.

(19) **FUT appears on direct object nominal, ACC on elements of relative clause (Lardil)**

Ngada	kurri-thu	karnjin-ku	[ngithun	thabuji-kan-i
I	see-FUT	wallaby-FUT	my	older.brother-GEN-ACC

la-tharrba-Ø].
spear-NONFUT-ACC
'I want to see the wallaby that my older brother speared.'
(Richards 2007; 2013, 52 ex. (30))

This is prima facie evidence that VACC is indeed assigned to direct objects that are also assigned FUT. I propose that the relative clause, while not a general barrier to FA, is a barrier to the assignment of tense morphology—possibly because CP is a domain with its own tense properties.[7] As a consequence, FUT morphology that would otherwise overwrite VACC in the relative clause (and does overwrite it in its NP host) is not assigned in the first place, and undeleted VACC morphology is pronounced in the relative clause as a consequence.

This brief discussion of Lardil has been useful to our investigation of Russian in several ways. First, it has shown that case stacking may be overt— so it is not entirely implausible to propose that it occurs covertly in a language such as Russian. Second, we have seen that the morphology of overt case stacking in Lardil reflects the derivation in just the manner that a proposal such as FA predicts: morphology assigned by lower heads occurs inside morphology assigned by higher heads. Finally, examples like (19) give us some reason to think that the factor that explains the covertness of case stacking in Russian, the One-Suffix Rule, is not an ad hoc proposal limited to Russian, but operates even in a language like Lardil that shows case stacking. Lardil deletes ACC morphology when it is not outermost, just as we have posited for Russian case morphology. What makes Lardil a "case-stacking language" is not the absence of the One-Suffix Rule, but the existence of undeletable suffixes that do not undergo the rule.

Lardil case stacking will be become important once again in chapters 8 and 9, when we discuss a puzzle posed by the morphology of genitive-marked adnominals in Russian. At that point, we will also take up a Lardil puzzle posed by the possessor of the genitive subject of the relative clause in (19) ('*my* older brother'). Given what we learned from examples like (14a–b), we expect this possessor to show VACC as well as NGEN morphology, reflecting the same assignment of VACC by the higher verb that the morphology of the head noun reflects. We might even expect the possessor to show two occurrences of GEN itself, reflecting both the assignment of NGEN to the possessor by the possessee and the assignment of NGEN to the subject DP that contains the possessor. Yet all we see is a single instance of genitive morphology. When we return to this problem, I will suggest that it too might have a counterpart in Russian; but I leave it as a loose end for now.

3.3 Interim Conclusions

In this chapter, I have shown how an analysis of Russian as a "secret case-stacking language" might handle the most straightforward facts about Russian case morphology. I have argued that such an analysis is not completely implausible with a brief discussion of Lardil, an overtly case-stacking language that seems to invite an analysis in very similar terms.

On the other hand, I have not yet even one empirical argument from Russian for any aspect of my proposal. I have presented no argument for the view that Russian nouns are born genitive; nor for the view that nominative case is assigned by D on top of genitive; nor for the claim that oblique case morphology is added by P outside previous nominative and genitive case marking. An argument that an analysis is "not completely implausible" may be a valuable first step—but it is very far from an argument that the analysis is *correct*.

In the remainder of this monograph, I will present two such arguments in depth, and I will situate them within a broader view of Russian case. These arguments center around the facts introduced in chapter 1 and related phenomena. If correct, they provide essential support for the proposals advanced here—and in turn suggest that the loftier goal discussed in chapter 2, the elimination of independent status for the case categories, might be achievable after all.

4 Argument 1 for the Core Proposal: NGEN, DNOM, and POBL

The first argument for the core proposal of this monograph concerns the case and number mismatches observed in chapter 1. I begin with a discussion of paucal constructions and then take up the differences between paucals and the nonpaucal numerals.

4.1 Number Mismatch with Paucals

As we saw in (1b), when an expression containing a nominative paucal such as *dva* 'two', *tri* 'three', or *četyre* 'four' combines with a noun, the noun shows morphology usually described as genitive singular. Example (20) shows the same phenomenon in simpler phrases that contain only the paucal and a noun.[1]

(20) **Paucal + N-GEN.SG (nominative environment)**
  a. dva   stol-a
     two   table-GEN.SG
     'two tables'
  b. tri   dnj-a
     three   day-GEN.SG
     'three days'
  c. četyre   stakan-a
     four   glass-GEN.SG
     'four glasses'

The use of the singular here is the feature characterized by Peškovskij (as quoted in the epigraph to this monograph) as a "typical example of the extent to which grammatical and logical thinking may diverge." In this chapter, I attempt to prove Peškovskij wrong, by arguing that a hidden logic underlies these facts after all.

The attractiveness of this challenge is enhanced by the number mismatch that appears when an attributive adjective is added to the right of the paucal.

As we saw, the adjective takes genitive *plural* morphology, in apparent disagreement with the noun's morphology, but in full agreement with the "logical thinking" about number seemingly absent from the noun.

(21) **A + N apparent number mismatch**
   Paucal + A-GEN.PL + N-GEN.SG (nominative environment)
   a. dva   nov-**yx**   stol-**a**
      two-NOM   new-GEN.*PL*   table-GEN.*SG*
      'two new tables'
   b. tri   solnečn-**yx**   dnj-**a**
      three-NOM   sunny-GEN.*PL*   day-GEN.*SG*
      'three sunny days'
   c. četyre   čist-yx   stakan-a
      four-NOM   clean-GEN.*PL*   glass-GEN.*SG*
      'four clean glasses'

Elsewhere in Russian, when an attributive adjective merges with a projection of N, its morphological number is determined by the number of the nominal expression that it modifies, as demonstrated in (22). If N is singular, the adjective is singular; and if N is plural, the adjective is plural.[2]

(22) **A + N number agreement**
   a. nov-yj   stol-ъ
      new-NOM.SG   table-NOM.SG
      'new table'
   b. nov-ye   stol-y
      new-NOM.PL   table-NOM.PL
      'new tables'

Can we show that the adjectives in (21) conform to the general pattern of (22), despite appearances, and display plural morphology for the same reason as their counterparts in (22): the plurality of the expression with which they have merged? This is not possible if one assumes the most obvious structure for the phrases of (21) stated as *hypothesis A* in (23), in which the adjective merges first with the noun, followed by the paucal, since in this structure the plural adjective has clearly not merged with a plural. Suppose instead, however, that the initial structure of the phrases in (21) actually conforms to *hypothesis B*, where it is the paucal that merges first with the noun, followed by the adjective.

(23) **Imaginable underlying structures for (21)**
   Hypothesis A: [paucal   [A   N]]
   Hypothesis B: [A   [paucal   N]]

In the structure associated with hypothesis B, though the bare noun is not plural, the *combination of noun and paucal* might count as plural for the purposes of adjectival agreement—in which case, adjectival number with paucals might conform to the general pattern after all. Let us therefore consider how hypothesis B might contribute to an overall solution to the various puzzles posed by paucal phrases.

Consider first the apparent number mismatch in examples like (21a–c). Even if hypothesis B can explain why the adjective is plural despite the absence of plural morphology on the noun, why does the noun lack plural morphology in the first place? The constituent structure of hypothesis B suggests a solution to the problem.

I propose that the noun in paucal constructions like (21a–c) is not singular at all, but *numberless*—entirely lacking the number feature (NBR)—and that the paucals are not numerals at all, but freestanding instances of NBR. A paucal, on this view, supplies a number specification for NP that would otherwise have entered the derivation as a property of the head noun.[3] If this proposal is correct, paucals like *dva*, *tri*, and *četyre* that are traditionally glossed as 'two', 'three', and 'four' are actually markers of *dual*, *trial*, and *quadral number*, respectively. (That is why I chose not to call these elements paucal *numerals*.) There is no number mismatch at all, just an alternation between periphrastic and synthetic ways of expressing nominal number.[4] On this view, the basic constituent structure of paucal constructions under hypothesis B is exactly the same as the constituent structure of a comparable example without a paucal, such as (22b). The sole difference lies in whether NBR is realized as part of the noun's morphology (added in the lexicon) or as a free morpheme (merged in the syntax).[5]

To be explicit, I propose that the grammar of Russian number has the syntactic and morphological properties listed in (24).

(24) **The NBR feature and its realization in Russian**
  a. *Feature geometry*
     The major featural distinction relevant to NBR is [±SINGULAR]. A Russian noun that is [−SINGULAR] may be additionally specified as DUAL, TRIAL, or QUADRAL, as warranted by the semantics of the expression in which it occurs.[6]
  b. *Low attachment*
     Only an N that has already combined with NBR may merge with other elements in the syntax. N may combine with NBR in one of two ways:

1. *Synthetically:* N enters the syntax already bearing NBR (because the nominalizer NGEN that formed the noun in the lexicon bears NBR); or

2. *Periphrastically:* N enters the syntax not bearing NBR (because the nominalizer NGEN that formed the noun does not bear NBR) and immediately merges with an instance of NBR.

In Russian, the only lexical items that bear DUAL, TRIAL, and QUADRAL number are the paucals, which are free morphemes. These morphemes select for N.

c. ***Morphological realization***

Russian case morphology makes a two-way number distinction, traditionally identified as "singular" versus "plural." If the proposals advanced here are correct, however, only the forms traditionally identified as "plural" unambiguously realize a particular number specification, namely, [−SINGULAR]. The forms traditionally identified as "singular" are actually *default* number forms, compatible with everything *except* [−SINGULAR]—crucially including both [+SINGULAR] and absence of NBR. That is:

Traditional designation	*If the present proposal is correct*
Plural morphology	[−SINGULAR]
Singular morphology	"Elsewhere" number (singular or absence of NBR)

The apparent number mismatch seen with paucals now disappears. An adjective that merges with N or with a projection of N simply agrees with the closest number-bearing element. (I return shortly to the case and number morphology of prepaucal nongenitive adjectives like *poslednie* 'last (pl.)' in example (1).) Since the paucal features DUAL, TRIAL, and QUADRAL are sub-features of [−SINGULAR] (and since these feature specifications are found only on paucals, which are exclusively adnominal), an adjective modifying a paucal phrase shows [−SINGULAR] number morphology, the morphology traditionally called "plural"—as illustrated in (25c), where the dual paucal exemplifies the periphrastic pattern also found with the trial and quadral paucals.

(25) **NBR features and NBR morphology**

a. *Synthetic singular NBR*

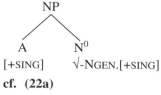

cf. **(22a)**

NBR morphology on A: default
(traditional name: *singular*)
NBR morphology on N: default
(traditional name: *singular*)

b. *Synthetic plural NBR*

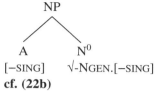

cf. **(22b)**

NBR morphology on A: [−SG]
(traditional name: *plural*)
NBR morphology on N: [−SG]
(traditional name: *plural*)

c. *Periphrastic dual NBR*

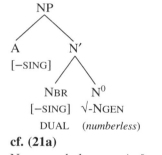

cf. **(21a)**

NBR morphology on A: [−SG]
(traditional name: *plural*)
NBR morphology on N: default
(traditional name: *singular*)

Before I proceed, a brief housekeeping note is necessary, in view of the nonstandard proposal advanced above. For compatibility with standard glossing conventions, I will continue to gloss the genitive form of N used with a paucal in a nominative environment as "singular"; but from this point on, I will annotate the gloss with a degree sign (i.e., GEN.SG°) when the present analysis would actually analyze the form as numberless (rather than singular). Where I wish to call special attention to numberlessness, however, I will mark the form in question explicitly as numberless.

4.2 Word Order and the Case Mismatch with Paucals

The proposal adopted above raises an obvious question concerning word order. The explanation offered for the apparent number mismatch between genitive

A and N in paucal constructions leads us to expect the order *A paucal N*, but the actual normal order is *paucal A N*, as in (21a–c).

(26) **Paucal precedes adjective**

    a.   dva   nov-yx   stol-a

          two.NOM   new-GEN.PL table-GEN.SG°

    b. *nov-yx   dva   stol-a[7]

If the present account of the apparent number mismatch is correct nonetheless, the contrast in (26) may be taken as evidence for obligatory leftward movement of NBR. I will argue that its landing site is D, as shown in (27).[8]

(27) **NBR-to-D movement**

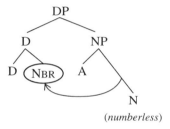

(*numberless*)

Of course, the word order problem could also be taken as an argument against the proposed account of the number mismatch, so it is important to seek independent evidence for the movement in (27). I will argue that the distribution of *case* in paucal constructions provides just such evidence—and that the movement in (27) resolves the second puzzle discussed in chapter 1: the *case mismatch*.

The viability of (27) as a component of the analysis of Russian paucal constructions presupposes, of course, that head movement exists more generally—a matter of some recent controversy. The well-known output structure for head-to-head movement proposed by Travis (1984) and supported by much subsequent work, (e.g., Baker 1988) in effect posits a *complement-creating* rule (though it is not usually described as such)—in that its input is a configuration of the form $[X^0\ YP]$ and its output is $[[X^0\ H]\ YP]$. (If Travis's Head Movement Constraint is correct, H is also the head of YP.) Let us call complement-forming movement *Undermerge*. Though the characterization of head-to-head movement as Undermerge is supported by the fact that X^0 and H behave as a constituent for later processes, it has caused some unease, because in this respect it does not resemble the instances of syntactic movement whose properties have been the most intensively studied (Matushansky 2006, 71), which are not instances of Undermerge. This concern has motivated numerous reanalyses of phenomena otherwise thought to involve

Undermerge-style head movement. One body of work has suggested, for example, that what looks like head movement might represent a chain of remnant phrasal movements instead (e.g., Koopman and Szabolcsi 2000; Mahajan 2000). Another approach accepts the existence of head movement, but argues that the moving head forms a (nonphrasal) specifier, not a complement—and thus behaves just like the better-accepted instances of movement (Matushansky 2006, and works cited there). According to this approach, what forms a constituent out of the moved head and its host is not the movement process itself, but a secondary, morphological process.[9]

Both of these alternative approaches are motivated (at least in part) by the belief that the apparent Undermerge property of head movement is not found with phrasal movement. Acceptance of the derived structure posited by Travis (1984), it is thought, thus entails acceptance of a property unique to head movement, rendering the analysis suspect. In fact, however, the literature does contain numerous strong arguments for complement-forming *phrasal* movement—so it is not a special demerit of the standard proposals for head movement that it too forms complements. McCloskey (1984), for example, offers an array of arguments for complement-forming movement to P in Irish. Likewise, Sportiche (2005) has argued that the D that appears on a DP argument of a verb is always generated as a head somewhere on the path between C and V, and joins with its NP by internal Merge (movement), rather than external Merge, as generally proposed (a proposal extended to Russian by Kondrashova and Šimík (to appear)). Sportiche's proposal has received additional support from the phenomenon of "determiner sharing" (McCawley 1993), as analyzed by Johnson (2000) and by Lin (2000)—as well as from arguments that the construction of negative DPs involves phrasal Undermerge of an NP to a negative head (Kratzer 1995; Penka 2001). Finally, of course, phrasal movement forming a complement of V ("Raising to Object") was proposed by Rosenbaum (1967) and defended by Postal (1974) and others.

It thus seems possible that Undermerge is a phenomenon as real and ubiquitous as movement to specifier position—and thus, that complement-forming head movement of the sort posited in (27) should not be rejected out of hand as an instance of an otherwise unattested process.[10] I will assume, therefore, that just as a head may require a particular specifier (an instance of the requirement often called EPP), which may be contributed by external or internal Merge, so a particular head may require a given *complement* as a lexical requirement—which also may be supplied by either internal or external Merge. For external Merge, such requirements have been familiar since Chomsky 1965 under the rubric of *subcategorization*. The present proposal, in effect, merely generalizes the notion of subcategorization so that such requirements may be satisfied by internal Merge as well. What governs the choice between complement formation and specifier formation to satisfy a given requirement, however, will remain an open question for internal Merge (just as it is for external Merge).[11]

Let us now return to the case mismatch found with paucal nominals in nominative environments. Since the paucals *dva* 'two', *tri* 'three', and *četyre* 'four' do have distinct genitive forms (*dvux*, *trëx*, *četyrëx*; see chapter 8), we can be sure that the paucals in examples like (21) show nominative morphology, while N and A are genitive.

If nominative morphology is D$_{\text{NOM}}$, its presence on the paucals in (21) is no surprise. Given the rule FA as formulated in (5), Undermerge of D with N$_{\text{BR}}$ is immediately followed by assignment of D$_{\text{NOM}}$ to N$_{\text{BR}}$. This formulation of FA, however, makes a wrong prediction about the morphology of A and N, since the earlier merger of D and NP should also have triggered assignment of D$_{\text{NOM}}$ to NP. Suppose instead that *only an element whose complementation requirements have been met qualifies as a feature assigner* (where "complementation requirements" include those satisfied by head movement as well as external Merge)—so that the correct formulation of FA is (28).

(28) **Feature Assignment (FA), version 2 of 6**
   a. *Copying:* When α merges with β, forming [$_α$ α β], *if α has satisfied its complementation requirements*, its grammatical features are immediately copied onto β ...
   b. *Realization:* ... and are realized as morphology on all lexical items dominated by β.

The new components of each revision of FA will be indicated with italics throughout this monograph.

Given (28), D in a configuration like (27) never assigns D$_{\text{NOM}}$ to NP. Since merger of D with NP did not satisfy D's complementation requirements, D could not assign D$_{\text{NOM}}$ at that point in the derivation. Ultimately, N$_{\text{BR}}$-to-D movement does satisfy D's complementation requirements (as an instance of Undermerge), but at that point it is too late for D to copy its morphology onto NP, since another Merge operation (internal Merge of N$_{\text{BR}}$) has intervened. As a consequence, N and A never receive D$_{\text{NOM}}$ morphology.

What morphology should N and A bear instead? Let us consider N first. If the reduction of case categories to parts of speech in (4) is correct, every noun enters the syntax bearing "primeval" N$_{\text{GEN}}$, as stated in (6). Consequently, if a noun in a paucal construction never receives D$_{\text{NOM}}$ (and if no other element copies its morphology onto the noun, the topic of the next section), we expect this noun to continue to show the overt N$_{\text{GEN}}$ morphology with which it entered the syntactic derivation.

Consider now the morphology of A in (27). FA entails that an element belonging to the category N not only *bears* NGEN, it also *assigns* NGEN—to any element that merges with it, immediately after Merge takes place. Furthermore, since feature assignment under (29) is not restricted to lexical heads, *any* element that merges with a projection of N should receive NGEN, not just elements that merge directly with the noun itself. Consequently, the adjective in (27) should receive NGEN from the N-headed constituent [*paucal* N] with which it merges, immediately upon merging with it. Once again, if D fails to assign DNOM to the NP that contains this adjective (because its complementation requirements are not yet met), the morphology we expect to see on the adjective is the NGEN morphology that it was assigned by the constituent [*paucal* N]—as is in fact the case.

Finally, consider the morphology that we expect to find on the paucal NBR. Since internal Merge of NBR to D does satisfy D's complementation requirements, we expect that D will assign DNOM morphology to the paucal, yielding precisely the case mismatch that we have observed between the nominative paucal and the genitive elements left within NP.

On this account, the genitive case found in paucal constructions is thus a kind of derivational "fossil," preserving NGEN morphology that would otherwise have been overwritten after merger with D. In this respect, the present account differs from most standard descriptions and previous accounts, in which the paucal does not prevent overwriting of a "primeval" genitive, but assigns it in the first place (e.g., Pesetsky 1982; Babby 1987; Franks 1995; Bailyn 2003).

The present proposal also accounts for the presence of DNOM morphology on prepaucal demonstratives and adjectives, a facet of the case mismatch puzzle first observed in (1b), repeated in (29). Since feature assignment is not restricted to lexical heads, once D has satisfied its complementation requirements by undermerging with the paucal, elements that merge with projections of D should also receive DNOM. This is exactly what we find.[12]

(29) **DNOM assigned by D′ as well as D**

    [DP **èt-i**   [D′ **posledn-ie**   [D′ D+   dv-**a**

       these-NOM.PL   **last-NOM.PL**   two-**M.NOM**

    [NP krasiv-**yx**   [t_{paucal} stol-**a**]]]]]

       beautiful-**GEN.PL**   table-**GEN.SG**°

    'these last two beautiful tables'

The proposal also predicts the contrast between paucal constructions and nominals that lack a paucal, such as (22a) or (22b). In such constructions, the complementation requirements of D *are* satisfied by merger with NP.

Consequently, Merge of D with NP in such cases *is* immediately followed by the assignment of DNOM to NP. In conformity with the One-Suffix Rule, DNOM morphology overwrites NGEN (both the primeval genitive morphology on N and the N-assigned genitive morphology on A), yielding a nominal all of whose dependents are morphologically nominative.

Note finally that the proposal presupposes a very particular logic behind the selectional requirement of D that triggers movement of the paucal in the constructions discussed so far. As examples like (1a) demonstrate, there is nothing wrong with a DP in which there is no independent NBR head. No element moves to D in such examples, and the result is the homogeneous pattern of DNOM morphology observed throughout the nominal phrase. On the other hand, whenever D is able to successfully probe for a freestanding paucal NBR, it does so—and acquires the selectional property that produces the nonhomogeneous case pattern and motivates movement of NBR to D. This is not the logic of probe-goal relations and movement first posited by Chomsky (2000, 2001) and widely adopted in subsequent literature; but it is a logic that has recently been defended as a more adequate proposal by Preminger (2009, 2010, 2011) (under the slogan "Failure to Agree is not a failure"). Preminger (2010), for example, shows that in a Hebrew sentence in which the unvalued φ-features of T can probe and find a φ-bearing DP, this DP must raise to form Spec,TP—that is, a preverbal subject. When probing is unsuccessful, however, the result is not a failed derivation. Instead the finite verb bears default agreement morphology, and no element raises to preverbal position. If the proposal advanced so far is correct, it provides another instance of the same logic. In section 6.1, I will suggest that NBR actually moves to D in two steps, first moving to an element that I will call QUANT, and then pied-piping to D as a consequence of QUANT-to-D movement. Preminger's logic will remain, however, and will apply to both steps of movement.

The advantage of the present proposal so far lies in the fact that it attributes several otherwise distinct properties of paucal constructions in nominative environments to the consequences of D's requiring movement of freestanding NBR (when it is present)—so long as we make the crucial assumption that nominative case is DNOM and that genitive is NGEN. The same complementation requirement of D that blocks DNOM assignment to the NP remnant (which thus retains its primeval genitive morphology) also predicts the assignment of DNOM to NBR itself and to any elements later merged with projections of D—and simultaneously resolves the word order problem raised by the underlying structure posited for paucal constructions (which in turn explained the number mismatch). In the next section, I strengthen the argument by showing that the disappearance of case mismatch in oblique environments seen first in (3) is also predicted by the analysis.

4.3   Paucal Constructions in Oblique Environments and the Role of Agree

I have suggested that a DP of the type seen in (21) shows a case mismatch because D has a second complementation requirement that motivates Under-merge of the paucal to it—leaving its first complement, the NP, unable to receive DNOM morphology. What if this DP is itself now merged with a new morphology-assigning head that does *not* have an unsatisfied complementation requirement? Consider, for example, the configuration in (30), in which a preposition has been merged to the DP in (27).

(30) **Merging P to (27)**

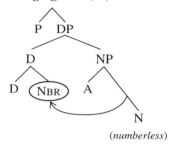

(numberless)

Suppose that P has oblique case morphology of its own to assign (e.g., PDAT) and that P (unlike D) has no second complementation requirement that motivates head movement to it. Such a P should uniformly assign its morphology to all the terminal elements of DP. Furthermore, given the One-Suffix Rule, the new morphology assigned by P should suppress the pronunciation of all previously assigned case morphology, including both DNOM on NBR and NGEN on the adjective and noun. As a consequence, the case mismatch should disappear, and the paucal, all adjectives, and the noun should uniformly show the morphology that P has assigned. This prediction is correct, as we saw in (3b) and similar examples in (31).

(31) **DPs with a paucal in a dative environment**

   a. (k)   dv-um   xoroš-im   stol-am
      to   two-DAT.PL   good-DAT.PL   table-DAT.PL

   b. (k)   tr-ëm   solnečn-ym   dnj-am
      to   three-DAT.PL sunny-DAT.PL   day-DAT.PL

   c. (k)   èt-im   posledn-im   četyr-ëm   krasiv-ym
      to   these-DAT.PL last-DAT.PL   four-DAT.PL   beautiful-DAT.PL

      stakan-am
      glass-DAT.PL

This "homogeneous" case pattern found in oblique environments is a much-discussed problem of Russian syntax, which has almost always been taken to motivate special stipulations about oblique nominals (Pesetsky 1982; Freidin and Babby 1984; Babby 1987; Franks 1995). In the present account, however, the homogeneous case pattern follows from the independently motivated One-Suffix Rule and the independent, banal fact that PPs are built by first constructing a DP and then merging a P.

The phrases in (31) are not merely homogeneous in case, however. They are also homogeneous in *number*, a fact not predicted by the proposal so far. The case suffixes of the terminal elements in (31) are all plural, in contrast to the "number mismatch" seen in (21), where only the adjectives were plural (more accurately, [−SINGULAR]). This is not a peculiarity of dative case. Other oblique case environments show exactly the same pattern.

(32) **DPs with a paucal in instrumental and prepositional environments**
   a. (s)   tr-emja   solnečn-ymi   dnj-**ami**
      with   three-INSTR.PL   sunny-INSTR.PL   day-INSTR.**PL**
   b. o   dv-ux   xoroš-ix   stol-**ax**[13]
      about   two-PREP.PL   good-PREP.PL   table-PREP.**PL**

The most obvious puzzle in these phrases is the plural morphology on N. If N in constructions like (21) is numberless, as argued in the previous section, the [−SINGULAR] feature of the case morphology found on N in (31)–(32) must be a property of the case morpheme itself—not a reflection of the features of the N to which it attaches. If this case morphology is simply a copy of the grammatical features of P, it must be P itself that comes to bear plural features in the presence of a plural complement (and singular otherwise).

We thus conclude that prepositions (both null and overt) bear an unvalued, presumably uninterpretable number feature (uNBR[ ], in the notation of Pesetsky and Torrego 2007, which receives its value by acting as a probe and triggering Agree with the closest bearer of valued NBR. In (30), this will set the value of NBR on P to [−SINGULAR]. The process of realizing the features of P that have been affixed to N (as well as those affixed to A and NBR) will thus take into account not only the properties of P that distinguish among dative, prepositional, and instrumental cases, but also the feature [−SINGULAR].

At this point, we should note (because this matter will be important later) that when a noun enters the syntax not numberless (as in the paucal constructions just discussed), but prevalued as singular or plural, the shape of case morphology assigned to it by FA reflects the *noun's own lexical value for*

NBR—not the NBR value of the assigner. Thus, for example, when a conjunction of singular nouns produces a constituent that agreeing elements (such as adjectives) treat as a plural, the morphology on each conjunct will be singular, even though the morphology on elements that agree with the conjunction as a whole is plural.

(33) **DNOM morphology on a conjunction of singulars and plural agreeing elements**
  a. *Nominative*
        mo-**i**   dorog-**ie**   [syn-**ъ**   i   dočk-**a**]
        my-NOM.**PL** dear-NOM.**PL** son-NOM.**SG** and daughter-NOM.**SG**
  b. *Dative*
        (k)   mo-**im**   dorog-**im**   [syn-**u**   i
        to   my-DAT.**PL** dear-DAT.**PL** son-DAT.**SG** and
        dočer-**i**]
        daughter-DAT.**SG**

The number value of the assigner of morphology under FA is decisive only in cases like the paucal construction, where the noun itself fails to bear a value for NBR.

(34) **How the NBR specification of case morphology is determined**
  Morphology assigned by α to β under FA reflects
  a. the NBR value of β if β is valued for NBR, and
  b. the NBR value of α otherwise.

Let us now review the discussion so far. The number mismatch between adjective and noun in a nominative paucal construction motivated a structure that, left to its own devices, incorrectly predicts the order *A paucal N*. The proposal that NBR moves to D solves this problem, yielding the correct order *paucal A N*, and simultaneously entails a derivation in which the complementation requirements of D are not met until a point at which it is too late for D to assign DNOM to the terminal elements of NP (assuming FA as formulated in (29)). Only the paucal and those elements that merge with higher projections of D are predicted to receive DNOM from D—a correct prediction. The remainder of the NP continues to bear "primeval" NGEN morphology—once again, a correct prediction. Finally, the proposal also correctly predicts that a higher assigner such as P should overwrite both nominative and genitive in DP with oblique morphology. Finally, it should be possible in principle for the number value of the morphology assigned by an element such as P to be determined by Agree, and this appears to happen as well.

Though the proposal does explain the case and number mismatches introduced so far, at least one key claim that lies at the heart of the story has not
been supported by any independent evidence: the proposal that the paucal
originates *low* in the nominal phrase (in fact, as a sister to N) and ends up *high*
(merged with D) only as a consequence of movement. It is the initial low
position of the paucal that explains the apparent number mismatch, and its
later high position undermerged to D that helps explain the case mismatch. It
would be reasonable at this point to ask for independent evidence of the proposed disparity between the underlying low position and the surface high
position of paucals. In the next chapter, I will present evidence of just this sort.
I will argue that a quirk of adjectival gender agreement provides independent
support for the low initial Merge position of paucals within a nominal phrase.

5 An Independent Argument from Gender Agreement for the Initial Low Position of Paucals

5.1 Gender, Noun Class, and Gender Mismatch

Russian distinguishes three grammatical genders: masculine, feminine, and neuter. The gender of a noun or nominal phrase can be detected by agreement patterns of the sort found in many Indo-European languages. In Russian, gender agreement is found with predicative and attributive adjectives, with demonstratives and relative pronouns, as well as with verbs inflected for past tense (historically descended from participles). For nouns denoting nonhumans, gender is almost always predictable from declension class, with only a small number of exceptions (mostly systematic). Nonhuman nouns of declension class 1 such as *stol* 'table' trigger masculine agreement—except for those whose nominative singular ending is *-o*, which are neuter. Nonhuman nouns of declension class 2 such as *lampa* 'lamp' trigger feminine agreement, as do most inanimates of declension class 3 such as *tetrad'* 'notebook'.[1]

Nouns that denote humans behave somewhat differently. Though feminine agreement is the norm for nouns of class 2, as just discussed, when a noun of this category unambiguously denotes a male human, it is always treated as masculine. Examples include *djadja* 'uncle', *deduška* 'grandfather', and a large class of male hypocoristics such as *Vanja* (< *Ivan*), *Kolja* (< *Nikolai*), and *Volodja* (< *Vladimir*), all of which consistently trigger masculine agreement. Furthermore, nouns of class 2 that denote humans without specification of sex are obligatorily treated as masculine in gender when they refer to men (or to individuals whose sex is unimportant to the context) and as feminine when they refer to women. Examples include *sirota* 'orphan', *plaksa* 'crybaby', *pjanica* 'drunkard', *sudja* 'judge', *brodjaga* 'vagabond', and many others (the

This chapter owes its existence to a conversation with Liudmila Nikolaeva, who raised the question of (45b) and its possible relevance to the analysis of paucals in this monograph.

class that Crockett (1976, 69ff.) calls *epicenes*). A class 2 noun that triggers masculine agreement behaves syntactically like any other masculine noun.

The phenomenon of interest to us, however, is a more complex agreement pattern found when a noun of class 1, a class that otherwise triggers masculine agreement, is used to refer to a female human. The most common examples of this sort are profession-denoting nouns such as *vrač* 'doctor', *professor* 'professor', *fotograf* 'photographer', *avtor* 'author', and many others. When a noun of this type is used to refer to a woman, it may trigger feminine, rather than masculine, agreement on adnominals such as adjectives and demonstratives. It may also trigger feminine subject agreement on past tense verbs and predicative adjectives. Unlike the class 2 pattern discussed in the previous paragraph, however, this type of sex-determined gender agreement is *optional*—and subject to several significant constraints that will preoccupy us below. It is these constraints that will shortly provide an independent argument for the low initial position that we have posited for paucals.

Consider first a sentence in which a noun like *vrač* 'doctor' is used to refer to a woman and appears with both an adnominal adjectival modifier and a past tense main verb. In constructions of this sort, the adjective and verb may show either masculine or feminine agreement.[2] Crucially, however, not all combinations are possible. In particular, though the verb may be feminine while the adjective remains masculine, feminine adjectival agreement entails feminine agreement on the verb, as shown in (35).[3]

(35) **Feminine adjective → feminine main verb with *vrač* 'doctor' with female referent**

a.	Nov-**yj**	vrač-ъ	prišël-**ъ**.	[✓ masculine adjective,
	new-**M**.NOM.SG	doctor-NOM.SG	arrived-**M**.SG	masculine verb]
b.	Nov-**yj**	vrač-ъ	prišl-**a**.	[✓ masculine adjective,
	new-**M**.NOM.SG	doctor-NOM.SG	arrived-**F**.SG	feminine verb]
c.	*Nov-**aja**	vrač-ъ	prišël-**ъ**.	[* feminine adjective,
	new-**F**.NOM.SG	doctor-NOM.SG	arrived-**M**.SG	masculine verb]
d.	Nov-**aja**	vrač-ъ	prišl-**a**.	[✓ feminine adjective,
	new-**F**.NOM.SG	doctor-NOM.SG	arrived-**F**.SG	feminine verb]

Furthermore, not all adnominal adjectives may bear feminine agreement when modifying a noun such as *vrač*. As Crockett (1976, 95ff.) discusses (developing an observation by Skoblikova (1971, 183)), feminine agreement is impossible with the kinds of adjectives that cross-linguistically appear at the lowest levels of the nominal phrase—those that have nonintersective, idiomatic, or argumental interpretation.

(36) ***Feminine agreement on *low adjective* modifying *vrač*-class noun with female referent**

    a. Glavn-**yj**/*Glavn-**aja**   vrač-ъ   poliklinik-i
       head-**M**/***F**.NOM.SG   doctor-NOM.SG   clinic-GEN.SG
       skazal-a,   čtoby ...
       say-PST.F.SG   that.SUBJ ...
       'The (female) head doctor of the clinic ordered that ...'

    b. Klassn-**yj**/*Klassn-**aja**   rukovoditel'-ь   soobščil-a
       class-**M**/***F**.NOM.SG   supervisor-NOM.SG   inform-PST.F.SG
       Česnokovu,   čto ...
       Chesnokov.DAT.SG   that
       'The (female) class supervisor informed Chesnokov that ...'

    c. Priiskov-**yj**/*Priiskov-**aja**   sčetovod-ъ   ser'ëzno
       mine.**M**/***F**.NOM.SG   accountant-NOM.SG   seriously
       zabolel-a.
       take.ill-PST.F.SG
       'The (female) mine accountant took seriously ill.'
       (Crockett 1976, 95–97)

(See Asarina 2008 for some suggestions concerning the semantic roots of this contrast.)

As Crockett also observes, when a low adjective cooccurs with high adjectives (or possessive pronouns) that do allow feminine agreement, many speakers even allow a DP-internal gender mismatch in which a low adjective is masculine, while higher modifiers are feminine.

(37) **High/Low gender mismatch: [FEM [MASC ...]]**

    a. V   17—očen'   xoroš-**aja**   glavn-**yj**
       in   17   very   good-**F**.NOM.SG   head-**M**.NOM.SG
       vrač-ъ ...
       doctor-NOM.SG ...
       'In [maternity hospital] no. 17 there is a very good (female) head doctor ...'
       (http://www.babyblog.ru/user/gorokha/665647, accessed March 20, 2010)

b. U   nas   byl-a   očen'   xoroš-**aja**
   by   us   COP-PST.F.SG   very   good-**F**.NOM.SG
   zubn-**oj**   vrač-ъ.
   dental-**M**.NOM.SG   doctor-NOM.SG
   'We had a very good (female) dentist.'
   (Skoblikova 1971, 183; also cited in Crockett 1976, 97)

c. Moj-**a**   nov-**aja**   klassn-**yj**
   my-**F**.NOM.SG   new-**F**.NOM.SG   class-**M**.NOM.SG
   rukovoditel'-ь   vsë   pričital-a ...
   supervisor-NOM.SG   ITER   complain-PST.F.SG
   'My new (female) class supervisor continually complained
   (that) ...'
   (http://detochka.ru/forum/index.php?showtopic=19618&st=30,
   accessed September 14, 2008)

A similar mismatch is also marginally possible internal to a group of high
adjectives, though I have found no speaker who accepts such examples without
qualms. Still, there is a crucial contrast. Though an outer high *feminine* adjective may marginally cooccur with an inner high *masculine* adjective, the
opposite pattern is completely excluded. Once a feminine adjective is used to
modify a nominal, any higher adjective must also be feminine.

(38) **High/High gender mismatch: ?[FEM [MASC ...]] vs.**
     *[MASC [FEM ...]]

a. ?U   menja   očen'   interesn-**aja**   nov-**yj**
      by   me   very   interesting-**F**.NOM.SG   new-**M**.NOM.SG
   vrač-ъ.
   doctor-NOM.SG
   'I have a very interesting new (female) doctor.'

b. *U   menja   očen'   interesn-**yj**   nov-**aja**
      by   me   very   interesting-**M**.NOM.SG   new-**F**.NOM.SG
   vrač-ъ.
   doctor-NOM.SG
   'I have a very interesting new (female) doctor.'

A simple derivational generalization may be extracted from all the patterns seen in (35)–(38). *Every nominal headed by a class 1 noun like* vrač *always enters the syntax masculine, but may be "feminized" in the course of the syntactic derivation.* Feminization is optional and may occur at any one of several points—but once it occurs, it is irreversible. That is why DP-internal (adjective-noun) feminine agreement entails DP-external (subject-verb) agreement, but not vice versa, as seen in (35). It is also why inner-adjective feminine agreement entails outer-adjective feminine agreement, but not vice versa, as seen in (38). Furthermore, *feminization may not occur "too early"* in the derivation of a nominal. In particular, it may not precede the merger of low adjectives, as (36) and (37) show.

5.2   The Feminizing Head Ж

I propose that "feminization" is the consequence of the adnominal merger of a phonologically null morpheme whose denotation is 'female' and whose properties are given in (39). I will represent this morpheme with the Cyrillic letter Ж (pronounced "že"), the first letter of *ženščina* 'woman' and many related words. The diagram in (40) shows where Ж may and may not merge, on this analysis, as summarized in (39).

(39) **Analysis of feminine agreement with *vrač*-class nouns**
   a. An optional null morpheme Ж 'female' may be merged at *any point above a certain structural threshold* within NP. Low adjectives fall below this threshold.
   b. Once Ж merges, the nominal counts as feminine for agreement purposes from then on.[4]

(40) **Possible Merge sites for Ж**

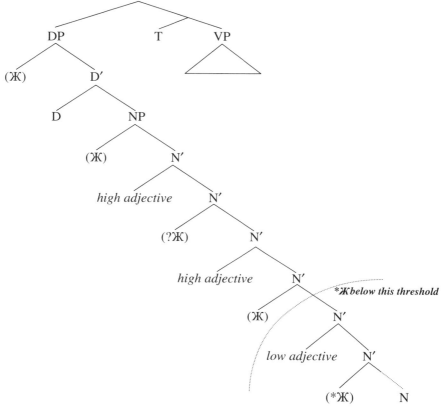

Let us now consider how this proposal accounts for the patterns of gender agreement that we have observed. The differing patterns of agreement in (35b) and (35d) reflect the difference between merging Ж above and merging Ж below the single high adjective. The unacceptability of (35c) results from the fact that feminine agreement on the adjective indicates a Merge site for Ж below the adjective; but this renders the DP feminine by (39b) and should have triggered feminine agreement on the verb. The absence of any feminine agreement in (35a) indicates a derivation in which Ж was not merged at all.

(41) **Analysis of (35a–d)**

    a.   [$_{(M)}$ Nov-yj [$_{(M)}$ vrač-ъ]] prišёl-ъ.   [✓ masculine adjective, masculine verb]

    b.   [$_{(F)}$ Ж [$_{(M)}$ nov-yj [$_{(M)}$ vrač-ъ]]] prišl-a.   [✓ masculine adjective, feminine verb]

   c. *[$_{(F)}$ Nov-aja [$_{(F)}$ Ж [$_{(M)}$ vrač-ъ]]] prišël-ъ.   [* feminine adjective,
                                                    masculine verb]

   d.   [$_{(F)}$ Nov-aja [$_{(F)}$ Ж [$_{(M)}$ vrač]]] prišl-a.   [✓ feminine adjective,
                                                    feminine verb]

Gender mismatches between high and low adjectives as in (37) reflect a Merge site for Ж between the high and low adjectives. The marginally acceptable gender mismatch seen with a pair of high adjectives in (38a) likewise reflects a Merge site available between them.

(42) a. **Analysis of nominal in (37a)**

      [$_{(F)}$ xoroš-aja   [$_{(F)}$ Ж [$_{(M)}$ zubn-oj   [$_{(M)}$ vrač-ъ]]]]
        good-F.NOM   dental-M.NOM   doctor-NOM.SG

     b. **Analysis of nominal in (38a)**

      [$_{(F)}$ očen'   interesn-aja   [$_{(F)}$ Ж [$_{(M)}$ nov-yj   [$_{(M)}$ vrač-ъ]]]]
        very   interesting-F.NOM   new-M.NOM   doctor-NOM.SG

The unacceptability of (38b) results from the fact that since the lower of two high adjectives is feminine, Ж must have merged below both of them—but then the higher adjective should have been feminine as well. The unacceptability of the feminine variants of (36), however, reflects something different: *the ban on merger of Ж below the threshold marked in (40)*. It is this phenomenon that will now provide an independent argument that the initial position of paucals is extremely low within NP.

There are three paucals in Russian that show gender agreement: *dva* 'two', *oba* 'both', and *poltora* 'one and a half', whose feminine forms are *dve*, *obe*, and *poltory*, respectively. Gender agreement with these paucals is illustrated in (43) with the class 1 masculine noun *stol* 'table' and the class 2 feminine noun *lampa* 'lamp', in a nominative environment.

(43) **Gender agreement with paucals *dva* 'two', *oba* 'both', and *poltory* 'one and a half' (nominative environment)**

    a. dv-a/ob-a/poltor-a   stol-a
       two/both/1½-M.NOM   table-GEN
       'two/both/one-and-a-half tables'

    b. dv-e/ob-e/poltor-y   lamp-y
       two/both/1½-F.NOM   lamp-GEN
       'two/both/one-and-a-half lamps'

Recall now that the proposed account of the number mismatch between the noun and adjectives in paucal constructions relied on the following crucial premise: although the surface position of a paucal is high within DP (sister to

D), its initial position was extremely low (sister to N)—and in particular, *lower than the lowest position in which any adjective merges*. This description must be as true of low adjectives as it is of high adjectives, since low adjectives display the same apparent number mismatch with paucals as high adjectives do.

(44) **Number mismatch with paucals and low adjectives**
    a. dva   glavn-**yx**   vrač-**a**
        two.NOM   head-GEN.**PL**   doctor-GEN.**SG**°
        'two head doctors'
    b. tri   zubn-**yx**   vrač-**a**
        three.NOM   dental-GEN.**PL** doctor-GEN.**SG**°
        'three dentists'
    c. četyre   klassn-**yx**   rukovoditelj-**a**
        four.NOM   class-GEN.**PL**   supervisors-GEN.**SG**°
        'four class supervisors'

The fact that certain paucals have special feminine forms now permits us to test a key prediction of the proposal. If the initial Merge position of paucals is lower than the lowest initial Merge position for low adjectives, then a fortiori it also lies below the threshold for merger of Ж. Consequently, despite the high surface position of paucals, we expect feminine agreement with a class 1 noun to be impossible, all things being equal—even when the nominal refers to a female.

The prediction is confirmed. In a nominative environment, the feminine forms of paucals may not be used with nouns like *vrač*.[5]

(45) **No feminine agreement between paucal and *vrač*-class noun**
    (nominative environment)
    a. dva/oba/poltora   vrač-a
        two/both/1½.M.NOM.SG   doctor-GEN.SG°
        'two/both/one-and-a-half (male or female) doctors'
    b. *dve/*obe/*poltory   vrač-a
        two/both/1½.F.NOM.SG   doctor-GEN.SG°
        'two/both/one-and-a-half (female) doctors'

This account of the contrast in (45a–b), if correct, offers precisely the independent support that we sought for the structurally low initial Merge position of the paucals—a proposal that was in turn crucial to the account of the number and case mismatches with which this monograph began.

As an alternative, one might entertain the hypothesis that examples like (45b) are not excluded by this monograph's proposals concerning the initial

Merge position of paucals, but instead are excluded by some idiosyncratic prohibition on the cooccurrence of Ж and paucals. In principle, a simple experiment should be able to distinguish the hypotheses. Unfortunately, as I will now show, the experiment, though simple, cannot be performed because of independent idiosyncrasies of Russian morphology.

The proposed account of (45) not only permits Ж to cooccur with a paucal— it actually predicts that adnominals added to a DP like (45a) may be feminine, so long as they do not belong to the class of obligatorily low adjectives. Thus, in an example such as (46), if Ж is present where indicated, the high adjective and the demonstrative might both be feminine (and if Ж were merged later, the demonstrative might be feminine and the adjective masculine) even though the paucal is not feminine.

(46) **Gender of high adjectives above Ж in a paucal construction**

èt-i	dv-a	nov-yx	Ж vrač-a
these-(F?).NOM.PL	two-NOM	new-(F?).GEN.PL	doctor-GEN.SG°

'these two new (female) doctors'

The problem with this experiment is the fact that Russian morphology suppresses almost all gender distinctions in the plural. (I discuss the sole exception immediately below.) Since adjectives and demonstratives in paucal constructions are plural, for reasons discussed earlier, there is no way to check the gender of the adjective or demonstrative in examples like (46), so this prediction cannot be tested.

There is, however, another way to show that Ж may in principle cooccur with a paucal. Note first that the proposed account of the impossibility of (45b) entails that D does *not* bear an unvalued gender feature in Russian (unlike adjectives and demonstratives). The visible morphology on *dva* and *oba* in (45a) is DNOM, copied from D by the rule FA. Consequently, *D must not undergo gender agreement*. Otherwise, in the presence of Ж, it would be feminine and would copy a *feminine* version of its morphology onto the paucal, incorrectly deriving (45b). The logic of this possibility would be the same as that underlying the proposed explanation for the plural oblique case morphology in (31) and (32), where P assigns the plural variant of its morphology to the terminal elements of DP as a consequence of number agreement with its complement.

On the other hand, the proposed account predicts that if a version of the DP in (45a) that includes Ж is merged with a higher head that *does* bear unvalued gender features, this higher head will copy a feminine version of its grammatical features onto all the terminals of DP—including the paucal itself. In such an environment, we *would* see a feminine paucal with a noun like *vrač*, providing an argument against any independent restriction on such a combination.

In fact, as I will now argue, Russian POBL appears to be a head of the desired type, behaving just as we expect from a category that bears an unvalued gender feature in addition to its unvalued number features. Given the general suppression of gender distinctions in the plural, it might seem impossible to tell whether a paucal inside a DP complement to POBL is masculine or feminine, since it will be plural. By a stroke of luck, however, one of these two paucals, *oba* 'both', has another idiosyncrasy that makes this test possible. *Oba* is the sole lexeme in the entire Russian language that distinguishes masculine and feminine forms in the plural. The other paucals, including *dva* 'two', do not, as (47) exemplifies.

(47) **Gender distinctions in the plural**

		Masculine				*Feminine*	
a.	(k)	ob-**o**-im	stol-am	b.	(k)	ob-**e**-im	lamp-am[6]
	to	both-**M**-DAT.PL	table-DAT.PL		to	both-**F**-DAT.PL	lamp-DAT.PL
c.	(k)	dv-um	stol-am	d.	(k)	dv-um	lamp-am
	to	two-DAT.PL	table-DAT.PL		to	two-DAT.PL	lamp-DAT.PL

When an oblique DP like those in (47a–b) contains a noun like *vrač* and the paucal *oba* 'both', and refers to a female, the paucal may indeed appear in its feminine form, in direct and striking contrast to (45b).

(48) **Feminine forms of *dva/oba* 'two/both' with *vrač*-class noun (oblique environment)**

a.	(k)	ob-**e**-im	vrač-am
	to	both-**F**-DAT.PL	doctor-DAT.PL
b.	(s)	ob-**e**-imi	vrač-ami
	with	both-**F**-INSTR.PL	doctor-INSTR.PL
c.	ob	ob-**e**-ix	vrač-ax
	about	both-**F**-PREP.PL	doctor-PREP.PL

As shown schematically in (49), in (48a–c) the paucal merged too early to agree in feminine gender with Ж, and (since D does not undergo gender agreement) received masculine DNOM morphology from D after movement. When P merged with DP, it agreed with the feminine gender introduced by Ж and with the plural number introduced by the paucal—and then copied feminine plural POBL morphology onto *oba*, suppressing previous masculine DNOM morphology (and onto *vrač*, surpressing previous numberless NGEN morphology).

(49) **P copies feminine, plural P<small>OBL</small> morphology onto** *oba* **and** *vrač*

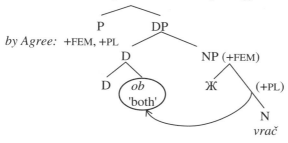

The feminine forms of *oba* are, of course, optional here, reflecting the optionality of Ж itself, and it is not possible to determine from (48) exactly where in the DP the morpheme Ж has merged. What the possibility of (48a–c) does make clear, however, is that Russian imposes no general ban on the cooccurrence of Ж and a paucal. This conclusion supports the account provided here for the unacceptability of (45b), which in turn supports the general proposal concerning the low origin of paucals within NP—one of the empirical foundations of the entire proposal.[7]

5.3   Gender Mismatch Is a Structural Phenomenon: Number in Lebanese Arabic

The strength of the argument just presented rests on the idea that the gender mismatches found with *vrač*-class nouns is the result of simple agreement processes that reflect an optionality in the use and Merge position of a feature-bearing head. One might question the purely syntactic nature of this account (and with it, its appropriateness as a tool for probing the initial Merge position of paucals) and posit instead some generalization more tightly connected to the semantics of feminine gender or the morphology of Russian declensional class.

   For this reason, it is useful to end this chapter with a brief discussion of a striking "twin" to Russian gender mismatches that has been uncovered by Ouwayda (to appear) in Lebanese Arabic number marking. As we will see, the logic of plural agreement in a subclass of Lebanese Arabic nominals with numerals is identical in virtually every respect to the logic of the gender mismatches that we have just discussed in Russian—and is amenable to an entirely parallel analysis. Ouwayda's findings provide a strong argument in favor of the construction-independent, purely syntactic approach that we have taken to their Russian counterparts, since the common denominator of the two phenomena is the logic of their syntax, not the specific semantic features or morphological quirks that interact with it.

Verbal number agreement with singular and plural subjects is straightforward in Lebanese Arabic when the subject lacks a numeral, or includes a numeral lower than 10, as (50) shows. Unsurprisingly, the noun bears plural morphology and the verb shows plural agreement with its subject.

(50) **Subject-verb agreement for number (Lebanese Arabic)**
    a. l-walad   daras   / * daras-u
       the-child.SG   studied.SG /   studied-PL
    b. l-wleed   daras-u   / * daras
       the-child.PL   studied-PL /   studied.SG
    c. tlat   wleed   / * walad   daras-u   / * daras
       three child.PL /   child.SG   studied-PL /   studied.SG

A more intricate and surprising agreement pattern is found, however, with nominals that include a numeral higher than 10 (and certain quantifiers). In such constructions, the noun obligatorily bears *singular* morphology.

(51) **Singular noun with numeral > 10 (Lebanese Arabic)**
    tleetiin   walad   / * wleed
    thirty   child.SG /   child.PL

I will not offer an analysis of this contrast (despite its family resemblance to the complexities of Russian numerals), but follow Ouwayda in focusing on its interaction with subject agreement. When a nominal like that in (51) is the subject of its clause, *it optionally triggers plural agreement* on the finite verb.

(52) **Optional plural subject-verb agreement with a subject containing a**
     numeral > 10 (Lebanese Arabic)
    [tleetiin   walad] daras-u   / daras
     thirty   child   studied-PL / studied.SG

The plural agreement option has semantic consequences, explored in detail by Ouwayda—permitting a collective interpretation for the nominal in addition to a distributive reading. Singular agreement allows only the distributive reading.

The same optionality of plural agreement is found inside the nominal phrase itself. A modifying adjective added to a nominal like (51) may be marked either singular or plural, as (53) shows. Note that the crucial nominal is a direct object in (53), so no issue of subject agreement arises yet.

(53) **Optional plural adjective agreement in a nominal containing a numeral > 10 (Lebanese Arabic)**

shefet	[tleetiin	walad	mnazzam	/	mnazzm-iin]
saw.1SG	thirty	child.SG	organized.SG	/	organized-PL'

'I saw thirty organized children.'

Crucially and remarkably, however, the patterns observed in constructions with more than one agreeing element mirror precisely the patterns observed for the feminine agreement option with *vrač* in Russian. When the adjective is singular and its nominal is the subject of a finite clause, the verb may be either singular or plural; but when the adjective is plural, the verb must be plural. Singular agreement becomes impossible. This is exactly the pattern of feminine agreement we saw in (35), with "singular" and "plural" substituting for "masculine" and "feminine."

(54) **Plural adjective → plural verb (Lebanese Arabic)**

a.
[tleetiin	walad	mnazzam]	daras	[✓ singular adjective,
thirty	child.SG	organized.SG	studied.SG	singular verb]

'Thirty organized children studied.'

b.
[tleetiin	walad	mnazzam]	daras-u	[✓ singular adjective,
thirty	child.SG	organized.SG	studied-PL	plural verb]

c.
*[tleetiin	walad	mnazzam-iin]	daras	[* plural adjective,
thirty	child.SG	organized-PL	studied.SG	singular verb]

d.
[tleetiin	walad	mnazzam-iin]	daras-u	[✓ plural adjective,
thirty	child.SG	organized-PL	studied-PL	plural verb]

Furthermore, when a nominal is modified by more than one adjective, number agreement mismatches among the adjectives are possible, but all singular adjectives must occur lower in the nominal than all plural adjectives—exactly the pattern we saw with Russian masculine versus feminine adjectives in (37)–(38).

(55) **Number mismatch with two adjectives: [[... SG] PL] vs. *[... PL [SG]] (Lebanese Arabic)**

a.
[tleetiin	walad	kesleen-Ø	mnazzam-iin]	Htajj-u
thirty	child.SG	lazy-SG	organized-PL	complained-PL

'Thirty organized lazy children complained (e.g., about their grades).'

b.
*[tleetiin	walad	kesleen-iin	mnazzam]	Htajj-u
thirty	child.SG	lazy-PL	organized.SG	complained-PL

Finally, as Sarah Ouwayda (personal communication) reports, low adjectives of the sort that disallow feminine agreement with Russian *vrač*-class nouns also disallow plural agreement in Lebanese Arabic nominals with numerals higher than 10. The number agreement contrasts in (56) are thus an exact counterpart to the Russian gender agreement contrasts in (36).

(56) **Plural agreement on *low adjective* in a nominal containing a numeral > 10 (Lebanese Arabic)**
  a. [tleetiin   mhandes   madani   / * madaniy-iin]
     thirty   engineer.SG   civil.SG   /   civil-PL
     'thirty civil engineers'
     (*plural acceptable with the high-adjective meaning 'thirty civilized engineers'*)
  b. [arbʔiin   tabiib   sharʔi   / * sharʔiy-iin]
     forty   doctor   legal.SG   /   legal-PL
     'forty forensic medical examiners'
     (*plural acceptable with the high-adjective meaning 'forty legal doctors'; for example, a clinic composed of 40 doctors who all have their licenses*)

The fact that a pattern of number mismatches identical to the pattern of Russian gender mismatches is found in an unrelated language suggests that a crucial presupposition of this chapter's discussion is correct. The logic of these mismatches is not due to specific morphological or semantic details of either language, but follows instead from the interaction between the Merge position of a morpheme and the construction-independent agreement rules that care about such morphemes.

For Russian, we attributed the choice of masculine or feminine gender agreement with a *vrač*-class nominal to the optional presence or absence of the feminine head Ж at several possible locations in syntactic structure. Exactly the same proposal is advanced by Ouwayda for Lebanese Arabic—with an optional pluralizing head # playing the same syntactic and morphological role that Ж plays in the present analysis of Russian, despite completely different semantics. The head # "triggers plural agreement on the verb, and … makes a collective reading of the noun available," with consequences for number exactly analogous to the consequences of Russian Ж for gender. Adjectives lower than # bear singular agreement, and adjectives higher than # bear plural agreement. Once # is present anywhere in a subject nominal, verbal agreement must be plural as well. Like Ж, Lebanese Arabic # may not be merged below a specific structural threshold: it may not come between a low adjective and the noun it composes with. The overall picture is illustrated in (57)—a tree structurally identical to the proposal for Russian summarized in (40).

(57) **Possible Merge sites for Lebanese Arabic #**

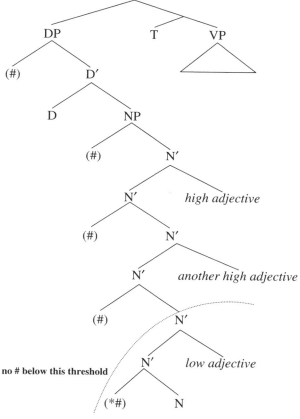

As we have seen, the semantics of Lebanese Arabic # are utterly different from the semantics of Russian Ж, and Lebanese agreement takes place against a syntactic background quite distinct from Russian as well (including post-nominal rather than prenominal adjectives)—yet the basic logic of the agreement mismatches is identical across the two languages. Ouwayda's discoveries provide crucial support for the purely syntactic nature of the tool we have used in this chapter, and thus for its plausibility as a means of detecting the initial Merge position of Russian paucals.

5.4   Conclusions

In this chapter, I have offered converging evidence from an entirely different domain for the proposal that Russian paucals originate in a very low position within their nominals and end up in their (relatively) high surface position as a consequence of movement to D.

In previous chapters, this proposal played a crucial role in explaining apparent number and case mismatches within such nominals. The paucal's movement to a high position, adjoined to D, helped explain the apparent case mismatch, by delaying and thus blocking the assignment of nominative by D to the rest of the NP. The paucal's initial low position was argued to reflect its status as a number marker, rather than a true numeral—thus explaining the absence of independent plural number morphology on the head noun. The analysis as a whole supports the broader view of case morphology defended in this monograph—as the copying of categorial features from heads to the elements they merge with, with genitive case viewed as the categorial features of N, nominative as the categorial features of D, and so on.

The high position of the paucal is evident from the position in which it is pronounced, but the proposal that its initial Merge position is low remained in need of independent support. This chapter has provided that support. Russian paucals behave exactly like the lowest of elements within NP when they interact with the feminizing morpheme Ж responsible for gender mismatches in *vrač*-class nouns (despite their high surface position). The proposed interpretation of this pattern received independent support of its own: namely, Ouwayda's discovery of the same pattern in Lebanese Arabic plural agreement. These Lebanese data should reassure us that the pattern does indeed reflect structural position, and not some factor specific to the morphology or semantics of Russian gender.

In the next chapter, I compare the behavior of Russian paucals with the behavior of high numerals and certain other quantifiers. As noted in chapter 1, nominals with these quantifiers share some of the properties of nominals with paucals. The discussion of these quantifiers, when combined with the further investigation of Russian case in chapter 7, will ultimately provide a second argument for the view of case developed in chapter 8.

6 Numerals and Other Quantifiers

6.1 The Category QUANT

As noted in chapter 1, there is a class of quantificational elements in Russian (henceforth **QUANT**) that show exactly the same pattern of case as that found with paucals, but not the same pattern of number. The QUANT class comprises the higher noncompound numerals through 100 (*pjat'* 'five', *šest'* 'six', etc.),[1] as well as a small group of nonnumeral quantifiers such as *mnogo* 'many', *nemnogo* 'a little', *stol'ko* 'so much', and *skol'ko* 'how much'. In a nominative environment, the head noun in constructions with these elements displays NGEN morphology, just as it does in constructions with paucals. The same is true of adjectives that appear to the right of QUANT, while (once again, just as in paucal constructions) an adjective or demonstrative that precedes QUANT displays DNOM—as does QUANT itself. The sole contrast with paucal constructions is the absence of any number mismatch. The head noun in constructions with QUANT is *plural*, as illustrated in (2), repeated here.

(58) **Quantificational construction (no paucal) (nominative environment)**
Case mismatch, but no "number mismatch"

èt-**i**	posledn-**ie**	pjat'-**ь**	krasiv-**yx**
these-**NOM.PL**	last-**NOM.PL**	five-**NOM**	beautiful-**GEN.PL**

stol-**ov**
table-**GEN.***PL*
'these last five beautiful tables'

In oblique environments, constructions with QUANT also behave like paucal constructions. Every element of the nominal expression displays POBL morphology, and both agreeing elements and noun are plural, as shown in (3c), repeated here.[2]

(59) **Quantificational construction (no paucal) (oblique environment, here PDAT)**

No mismatches

èt-**im**	posledn-**im**	pjat-**i**	krasiv-**ym**
these-**DAT.PL**	last-**DAT.PL**	five-**DAT**	beautiful-**DAT.PL**

stol-**am**
table-**DAT.PL**

'to these last five beautiful tables'

The case patterns in (58) and (59) may receive an explanation identical to that offered for the comparable patterns in paucal constructions, so long as we suppose that some element is required to move to D in examples like (58), to satisfy a requirement of D, just as in paucal constructions. From this point on (but not before), D assigns DNOM to each element that merges with D (or with a projection of D). The head noun and adjectives that remain within NP, however, will continue to bear NGEN—unless DP itself merges next as the complement of P, in which case all previous case morphology in the nominal will be overwritten by POBL, yielding the "homogeneous pattern" of (59).

But what *is* the element that moves to D in constructions like (58), if this analysis is correct? The obvious candidate is QUANT itself. Consider first what we know about the most likely initial Merge site for QUANT. For a numeral instance of QUANT, at least, the cross-linguistic investigations that have motivated and supported Greenberg's (1963) Universal 20 suggest that its initial Merge site is NP-internal and that its position in the NP is higher than that of all other NP-internal adjectives—and, of course, below D, since it is NP-internal (Cinque 2005).[3] The fact that the numeral bears DNOM morphology in constructions like (58), however, suggests that it undergoes movement from this NP-internal position to D (or to a projection of D). QUANT is thus a very plausible candidate for an element that moves to D just like the paucals that we have investigated in preceding chapters (as illustrated in (60))—with identical consequences for the distribution of case morphology in both nominative and oblique environments.

(60) **QUANT-to-D movement**

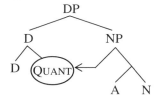

On the other hand, however similar the final position of QUANT might be to the final position of paucals, their initial positions are clearly not the same. I have argued at length that a paucal is an instance of NBR and that its initial Merge site is extremely low within N. A paucal is merged directly with a numberless N, thus supplying the NP with the grammatical number specification that other nouns receive in the lexicon—an apparent precondition for further merger to projections of N, as noted in (24b). By contrast, if the initial position of QUANT is governed by the principles behind Greenberg's Universal 20, its initial Merge site must be extremely *high* within NP. Given (24b) once again, this means that QUANT, unlike the paucals, does *not* merge to a numberless projection of N, but merges instead to a projection of a noun that has already been marked for number. Given the semantics of the elements in the QUANT class ('five', 'many', etc.), it is no surprise that the head noun in QUANT constructions is generally plural—not numberless as it is in paucal constructions. The absence of a seeming number mismatch in the QUANT construction is thus explained.[4]

This proposal now contains an odd disjunction, which should concern us. If the proposal is correct as stated so far, some feature of D must probe for an element that may belong to either of two distinct categories, QUANT and NBR. Can we avoid this conclusion?

A plausible alternative is in fact available, if we refine our view of the path by which NBR ends up in D in paucal constructions. I have assumed so far that paucal NBR moves to D in a single step, but this was not a necessary assumption. In particular, since QUANT is located between NBR and D, it is also possible that QUANT provides a landing site for NBR on its way to D. In particular, it is possible that NBR only moves in the first place because it is attracted by a feature of QUANT—and moves to QUANT, rather than to D. Since examples like (58) teach us that D, in turn, attracts QUANT, it is possible that NBR ends up in D not as a result of direct NBR-to-D movement, but as a consequence of pied-piping by QUANT when QUANT (not the paucal itself) is attracted by D. In other words: first NBR moves to QUANT, then when QUANT moves to D, it takes NBR with it, as shown in (61).

(61) **A two-step theory of how Nʙʀ ends up in D: Nʙʀ-to-Qᴜᴀɴᴛ**
       movement followed by Qᴜᴀɴᴛ-to-D movement

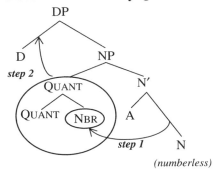

(numberless)

Note that step 2, in which Qᴜᴀɴᴛ pied-pipes Nʙʀ to D, is not dispensable. We
do know that the final position of paucal Nʙʀ is external to NP, because it ends
up bearing Dɴᴏᴍ—unlike the adjectives and noun left behind in NP, but just
like such Qᴜᴀɴᴛ elements as *pjat'* 'five' in (58).

What must we say about the distribution and properties of D and Qᴜᴀɴᴛ,
if the two-step proposal in (61) is correct? Let us begin by noting that not
every DP shows movement of Qᴜᴀɴᴛ to D. In a nominal that has neither a
paucal nor an overt instance of Qᴜᴀɴᴛ in it, no Qᴜᴀɴᴛ-to-D movement takes
place. That is why D in such a nominal assigns Dɴᴏᴍ to all the elements of
NP, as illustrated in (1a), repeated as (62).

(62) **No paucal, no Qᴜᴀɴᴛ: No movement to D, Dɴᴏᴍ throughout**
       (nominative environment)

èt-**i**	posledn-**ie**	krasiv-**ye**	stol-**y**
these-**NOM.PL**	last-**NOM.PL**	beautiful-**NOM.PL**	table-**NOM.PL**

       'these last beautiful tables'

I will assume that in constructions like these, Qᴜᴀɴᴛ is simply missing. This
entails that whatever feature of D probes for Qᴜᴀɴᴛ and attracts it to D when
it is found does not crash the derivation if Qᴜᴀɴᴛ is not found, but receives a
default value and does not require movement of any sort.

On the other hand, when dual, trial, or quadral Nʙʀ is present in an NP,
Qᴜᴀɴᴛ must also be present. Otherwise, Nʙʀ in a paucal construction would
be free to remain in its low base position, nothing would move to D, and D
would assign Dɴᴏᴍ morphology to all the elements of NP, contrary to fact.
Thus, if (61) is correct, something in the overall theory must entail that a
paucal obligatorily cooccurs with a null Qᴜᴀɴᴛ, and some feature of this null
Qᴜᴀɴᴛ must successfully probe and attract the paucal.

What this suggests is that a Russian nominal phrase that denotes two, three, or four of some entity *always* contains a genuine numeral of the QUANT class whose interpretation is 'two', 'three', or 'four'—just like phrases that denote a higher quantity of an entity, such as 'five'. The favored mode of expression for this numeral, however, is a null QUANT that comes from the lexicon unvalued for the features that permit it to denote a precise quantity. Null QUANT can be used in a nominal phrase when it is able to value its quantity features, which it may do if it enters into an Agree relation with an appropriate instance of NBR. In Russian, this is possible for just those quantities that have corresponding instances of NBR: namely, the paucals. It is when null QUANT cannot be valued in this way that the language resorts to QUANT words that come from the lexicon prevalued for the relevant features, including numerals like *pjat'* 'five' and the others mentioned above.

The Russian lexicon actually contains special overt forms of QUANT that denote 'two', 'three', and 'four' as well. As the proposal predicts, these are used primarily when the minimally differing structure with null QUANT is unavailable—which will happen when the kind of NBR that can provide a value to the features of QUANT is itself unavailable. One place where this situation arises is the domain of *pluralia tantum*: entity-denoting nouns idiosyncratically prespecified as plural in the lexicon (Pesetsky and Torrego 2007; Acquaviva 2008). Because a *plurale tantum* noun must be grammatically plural, it lacks the numberless form that a paucal requires. Since paucal NBR cannot be used with such a noun, null QUANT is also impossible, since it relies on NBR for valuation. Instead, a set of special numerals—*dvoe, troe,* and *četvero*—are used in nominative environments.[5] The claim that these numerals belong to the same class as QUANT numerals such as *pjat'* 'five' in (58) is supported by the fact that their syntax and interaction with case morphology are identical. Example (63) illustrates this with *sutki* '24-hour period', a *plurale tantum*. Note the presence of the characteristic case mismatch, and the absence of the "number mismatch" found with paucals (and null QUANT, in the analysis under discussion in this chapter).

(63) **Special low QUANT numerals with *pluralia tantum* (nominative environment)**

èt-**i**	posledn-**ie**	dvo-**e**	strašn-**yx**
these-**NOM.PL**	last-**NOM.PL**	two (QUANT)-**NOM**	terrible-**GEN.PL**
sutok-**ъ**			
24h-**GEN.PL**			

'these last two terrible days' (*any variant with paucal *dv-a*)

Certain other nominals regularly require these special QUANT forms for the
low numerals, arguably (in the context of the present proposal) because they
too lack a numberless form that can be used with dual, trial, or quadral freestanding NBR. One prominent category consists of those masculine nouns
denoting male humans that belong to the otherwise feminine declension class
2, such as *mužčina* 'man'. The forms otherwise expected (e.g., *dv-a mužčin-y
'two-M.NOM man-GEN.SG°') are disallowed, and a construction with the special
overt QUANT form of the low numeral once again must be used instead
(Mel'čuk 1985, 391; Yadroff 1999, 142).[6]

(64) **Special low numerals with masculine class 2 nouns (nominative
     environment)**

èt-**i**   posledn-**ie**   dvo-**e**   molod-**yx**
these-**NOM.PL** last-**NOM.PL**   two (QUANT)-**NOM** young-**GEN.PL**
mužčin-**ъ**
man-**GEN.PL**

'these last two young men' (*any variant with paucal *dv-a*)

The "last resort" character of the use of the special QUANT forms can also be
seen in the fact that when nominal phrases like (63) and (64) are used in an
oblique environment, where unpronounceable numberless NGEN morphology
on N is expected to be overwritten by plural POBL morphology, versions with
normal paucals (and null QUANT) are preferred over versions that include
special QUANT forms. The special QUANT form for 'two' with PDAT morphology would be *dvoim* rather than *dvum*.[7]

(65) **Paucal rather than special QUANT numerals in an oblique variant
     of (63)**

(k) èt-**im**   posledn-**im**   dvu-**m**
(to) these-**DAT.PL** last-**DAT.PL**   two (paucal)-**DAT**
strašn-**ym**   sutk-**am**
terrible-**DAT.PL** 24h-**DAT.PL**

'to these last two terrible days'

The existence of overt QUANT numerals for 'two', 'three', and 'four' lends
credence to the idea that QUANT *may* cooccur with the lower numerals. This
is a useful conclusion, because it supports a crucial precondition of the two-
step analysis of paucal constructions in (61) that requires the *obligatory* presence of this position in paucal constructions.

   We conclude that D uniformly attracts QUANT. Paucals that end up in D do
so by first moving to QUANT, and then moving to D as part of QUANT-to-D
movement.

This claim does not entail that QUANT is the only element that ever head-moves to D in Russian. Multiple head movement to D should, however, have an interesting property: DNOM should not be assigned until the final instance of movement takes place. As a result, elements that move to D early should not be assigned DNOM, but should retain NGEN morphology—unless it is overwritten by later applications of FA. Under these circumstances (and under these circumstances alone), we might see a phrase marked with NGEN, rather than DNOM, to the left of a nominative paucal or numeral in D.

One candidate might be the "modified cardinal construction" (Ionin and Matushansky 2004) studied by Crockett (1976, 345–347), Corbett (1979), and Babby (1985, 1987), among others. Here we appear to see exactly the kind of genitive phrase that the current proposal leads us to expect.

(66) **The modified cardinal construction: Genitive to the left of QUANT
      in D (nominative environment)**

dobr-yx   pjat'-ь   krasiv-yx   stol-ov
good(ly)-GEN.PL   five-NOM   beautiful-GEN.PL   table-GEN.PL
'a good five beautiful tables'

Only a small set of adjectives participate in this construction: *celyj* 'whole', *lišnij* 'extra', *polnyj* 'full', *nepolnyj* 'almost' (lit. 'incomplete'), and *kakie-nibud'* 'some', in addition to *dobryj* seen in (66). Semantically, as Crockett (1976, 346) notes, "the genitive attributes only modify the numerals—they are QP modifiers rather than NP modifiers" (see Solt 2007, building on Kayne 2005, for a related view of the English counterpart). To Crockett, this observation suggested a syntactic analysis in which these adjectives originate as modifiers of QUANTP. If we were to incorporate Crockett's proposal into the present analysis, NGEN on the adjective would reflect assignment of NGEN by N to a QUANTP sister to N'. Its plural number would result from QUANTP-internal agreement between the modifier and QUANT.

If QUANT head-moves on its own to D, however, as argued throughout this monograph, the word order poses a puzzle. On the relevant reading, *celyx* and the other adjectives under discussion do not appear to the right of the numeral (except as an uncommon, marked order; see Corbett 1979, 5 exx. (15)–(17)). If QUANTP moves as a whole to D, however, we wrongly predict that the QUANT-modifying adjective should receive DNOM alongside QUANT itself. The solution might be as follows: Both the QUANT-modifier and QUANT are separately attracted by D, in that order. Because the QUANT-modifier moves first, before D's requirement for QUANT is satisfied, FA does not apply, and DNOM is not assigned to it. Once QUANT moves next (tucking in below the

QUANT-modifier), the requirements of D are met, so DNOM is assigned to QUANT.

This proposal makes two correct predictions. First, if a demonstrative or adjective such as *poslednij* 'last' externally merges with a projection of D later in the derivation, it should receive DNOM, resulting in a superficially "super-heterogeneous pattern."

(67) **Super-heterogeneous nominal: Nominative to the left of modified cardinal construction**

Posledn-ie   cel-yx   sem'-ъ   let-ъ! —
last-NOM.PL   whole-GEN.PL   seven-NOM   years-GEN.PL
                    otdany polnometražnomu xudožestvennomu filmu ...
'The last whole seven years!—devoted to a feature film ...'
(http://www.novayagazeta.ru/data/2009/133/06.html, accessed March 10, 2013)

Second, in an oblique environment, the QUANT-modifier should receive the same oblique morphology as the rest of the DP. As Babby (1987, 124 n. 27) observes, this prediction is also correct. Though Franks (1995, 126 n. 16) reports that some speakers disagree with Babby's empirical claim, naturally occurring examples are common.

(68) **A super-heterogeneous nominal loses heterogeneity when oblique**

Tak u nas ved' uže est' kontrakty
[s   cel-ymi   pjat'-ju   krupn-ymi
 with   whole-INSTR.PL   five-INSTR   major-INSTR.PL
klient-ami],
client-INSTR.PL
             na naš vek xvatit.
'And after all, we already have contracts with a whole five major clients, enough to last our lifetime.' [from a text mocking the reasoning of certain naive advertising agencies]
(http://mmr.net.ua/issues/year/2007/num/4/news/164/, accessed August 26, 2010)

6.2   Quantifiers That Always Show a Homogeneous Case Pattern

Not all quantificational nominal phrases display the nonhomogeneous case patterns diagnostic of QUANT-to-D movement. In some cases, we can be fairly sure of the reason: the quantifiers in question are not instances of QUANT (nor elements that move to QUANT). Universal and generic quantifiers such as *každyj* 'every', *ves'* 'all', *vsjakij* 'any, every', and *ljuboj* 'any (free-choice)', for example, all display homogeneous case patterns in nominative environments.

(69) **Universal/Generic quantifiers with a homogeneous case pattern (nominative environment)**

    a. každ-yj   krasiv-yj   stol-ъ
       each-M.NOM.SG   beautiful-M.NOM.SG   table-NOM.SG
       'each beautful table'

    b. vs-e   krasiv-ye   stol-y
       all-NOM.PL   beautiful-NOM.PL   table-NOM.PL
       'all beautiful tables'

A universal quantifier in this group may also cooccur with a numeral, in which case the universal quantifier precedes the numeral. Like the prenumeral demonstrative and adjectives in examples like (1b) and (2), the universal quantifier bears DNOM morphology in a nominative environment. Such facts suggest that we are not dealing with an instance of QUANT; rather, we are dealing with a quantifier that is introduced as a sister to a projection of D, just like these prenumeral demonstrative and adjectives. In that position, D assigns DNOM to it as expected.

(70) **Evidence that the quantifiers of (69) are dependents of D**

    a. V učebnom grafike,
       každ-ye   pjat'-ь
       each-NOM.PL   five-NOM
       učebn-yx   nedel'-ь
       teaching (adj.)-GEN.PL   week-GEN.PL
                         zaveršajutsja kanikulami.
       'In the teaching schedule, every five teaching weeks concludes with a vacation.'
       (http://school10.cuso-edu.ru/images/material-images/2009.doc, accessed August 2, 2010)

    b. vs-e   pjat'-ь   krasiv-yx   stol-ov
       all-NOM.PL   five-NOM   beautiful-GEN.PL   table-GEN.PL
       'all five beautiful tables'

(71) **Structure of (70b)**

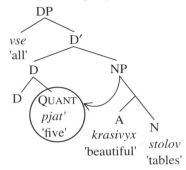

There are a few other cases where we also find a homogeneous case pattern in a quantified noun phrase. Examples in this category include phrases with *mnogie* 'many' and *nemnogie* 'a few', which function as doublets for the QUANT elements *mnogo* 'many' and *nemnogo* 'a few' (Rappaport 2002, 337). It is conceivable that these quantifiers are DP dependents, like *vse* 'all' in (71). If their semantics determines their initial position, however, they are more likely to be QUANT elements whose initial position is the same as that of their near-synonyms *mnogo* and *nemnogo*—but which fail to raise to D, because they lack the feature for which D probes.[8]

(72) **Homogeneous case pattern with *mnogie* 'many'**

S texničeskoj točki zrenija,

mnog-ie	krasiv-ye	motocikl-y
many-NOM.PL	beautiful-NOM.PL	motorcycle-NOM.PL

                                                          neudačny.

'From a technical point of view, many beautiful motorcycles are unsuccessful.'
(http://autopilot.kommersant.ru/issues/auto/2001/06/078.HTML, accessed August 2, 2010)

Similar issues arise for constructions with the word *odin*. This is the normal Russian rendering of the numeral 'one' when it functions as an adnominal, but it may also be used to mean 'alone', 'some' as opposed to 'others' (in its plural form)—and occasionally it has the force of the English indefinite article. Nominal phrases with *odin* (in any of its senses) also show a fully homogeneous case pattern in both nominative and nonnominative environments (as mentioned in chapter 1, note 2).

(73) **Homogeneous pattern with *odin* 'one'**

    a. *No mismatches (nominative environment)*

        odin-ъ   krasiv-yj   stol-ъ

        one-M.NOM.SG   beautiful-M.NOM.SG   table-NOM.SG

        'one beautiful table'

    b. *No mismatches (oblique environment)*

        odn-omu   krasiv-omu   stol-u

        one-M.DAT.SG   beautiful-M.DAT.SG   table-DAT.SG

        'one beautiful table'

Despite denoting a quantity lower than any paucal, *odin* is clearly not a paucal; that is, it is not an instance of NBR. The argument comes from its interaction with gender in the contexts discussed in chapter 5. Like *dva* 'two' and *oba* 'both' discussed there, *odin* shows gender agreement (in this case distinguishing all three genders). The argument in chapter 5 for the low initial Merge site of paucals came from the inability of *dva* and *oba* to show feminine agreement with class 1 nouns like *vrač* 'doctor' (and the independent observation that low adjectives share that inability). In contrast to the paucals, *odin* does allow feminine agreement with such nouns. This means that its initial Merge position is not the low position where paucal NBR is introduced, but is higher.

(74) **Feminine agreement between *odin* 'one' and *vrač*-class nouns**

    Byl-a   na   učastke   odn-a   xoroš-aja

    was-F.SG   on   district   one-F.NOM.SG   good-F.NOM.SG

    vrač-ъ,   tak   eë   uvolili.

    doctor-NOM.SG,   so   her   they.fired

    'There was one good (female) doctor in the district, so they fired her.'
    (http://blogs.mail.ru/mail/lisik-85/2CEA82BA9BD08D0D.html?thread=
    45FDC4013365EB02&skip=0, accessed July 31, 2010)

The fact that it may be used as a numeral suggests that *odin* too is an instance of QUANT that is not attracted to D, at least in its numeral use.[9] (If QUANT is the highest head within NP, the linear position of an element that remains in QUANT will be indistinguishable from the linear position of a QUANT that has moved to D.) On the other hand, its similarity in other uses to the English indefinite article might suggest that it is actually an instance of D, or a dependent of D like the universal and generic quantifiers considered above. Likewise, its ability to function as an adjective meaning 'alone' might group it with the adjectives. Any one of these proposals (or any combination of them) is compatible with the homogeneous pattern, and unfortunately I have no argument that settles the question.[10]

7 Vacc and the Morphosyntax of Direct Objects

7.1 Feature Assignment and Complements of V

Head movement to a feature assigner is not the only circumstance in which an expected application of FA is blocked, revealing a layer of case morphology that would otherwise have been overwritten. In this section, I will argue that certain categories of DP resist the assignment of Vacc as an idiosyncratic fact about the lexicon of Russian. The stipulative character of this phenomenon is irreducible, since it makes reference to Russian-specific properties of grammatical gender. Nonetheless, though the circumstances in which FA is blocked are peculiar to Russian (hence stipulated), the *consequences* of FA failure are exactly as predicted by the general theory proposed here, and thus actually provide additional support for it.

In the general case, the complements of transitive verbs in Russian bear morphology traditionally called "accusative." As in many languages, the complements of certain verbs are exceptions to this rule and idiosyncratically appear to bear oblique cases. Under the proposals presented here, these complements are actually PPs whose prepositional head is null. (Thus, for example, the verb *pomoč'* 'to help', which appears to take a DP complement marked with Pdat morphology, actually selects a PP complement whose head is a silent dative-assigning preposition.) I put this class of exceptional verbs aside, and focus on the verbs whose complements are normally regarded as accusative. The reason for my hedges "traditionally called" and "normally regarded" in describing the case properties of these complements will be made clear shortly.

In chapter 2, I suggested that accusative case morphology found on DP complements to transitive active verbs (like all case morphology) is a consequence of the assignment of Vacc by V, in conformity with the rule FA. In fact, however, though certain types of DPs do show distinct morphology in accusative environments, others appear in their *nominative* form. Strikingly, these DPs show no sign whatsoever of having undergone any morphology assignment by V. Every word of the complement DPs bears the same morphology otherwise found in a nominative environment. The types of DPs that have this property are shown in (75).

Particularly telling is the fact that the paucal and QUANT constructions in (75b–c) retain the "nonhomogeneous" pattern of case and (for paucals) number marking characteristic of nominative environments, despite their status as complements of V. This nonhomogeneous pattern should have been replaced by a homogeneous pattern, if V were assigning its own ACC morphology. The elements found in DPs that lack paucals and QUANT elements are likewise indistinguishable from their counterparts in nominative environments. It is for this reason that I gloss such forms as NOM here and elsewhere—reserving the designation "ACC" for forms distinct from the nominative.

We are clearly not dealing with mere syncretism between NOM and ACC, but with genuine NOM morphology in a position where we might have expected to see ACC.

(75) **DP complements to V that do *not* receive VACC morphology**

  a. *Inanimate masculine or neuter singular DP*

My	videli	ètot	krasiv-yj	stol-ъ.
we	saw	this.M.NOM.SG	beautiful-M.NOM.SG	table-NOM.SG (M)

  'We saw this beautiful table.'

  b. *Inanimate plural DP (any gender)*

Masculine noun

My	videli	èt-i	krasiv-ye	stol-y.
we	saw	these-NOM.PL	beautiful-NOM.PL	table-NOM.PL (M)

  'We saw these beautiful tables.'

Feminine noun

My	videli	èt-i	krasiv-ye	lamp-y.
we	saw	these-NOM.PL	beautiful-NOM.PL	lamp-NOM.PL (F)

  'We saw these beautiful lamps.'

  c. *Inanimate paucal construction (any gender)*

Masculine noun

My	videli	èt-i	dv-a	krasiv-yx
we	saw	these-M.NOM.PL	DUAL-M.NOM	beautiful-GEN.PL

stol-a.

table-GEN.SG° (M)

  'We saw these two beautiful tables.'

Feminine noun[1]

My	videli	èt-i		dv-e	krasiv-yx
we	saw	these-M.NOM.PL		DUAL-F.NOM	beautiful-GEN.PL

lamp-y.
lamp-GEN.SG° (F)
'We saw these two beautiful lamps.'

d. *Inanimate QUANT construction with QUANT-to-D movement (any gender)*

Masculine noun

My	videli	èt-i	pjat'-ь	krasiv-yx
we	saw	these-M.NOM.PL	five-NOM	beautiful-GEN.PL

stol-ov.
table-GEN.PL (M)
'We saw these five beautiful tables.'

Feminine noun

My	videli	èt-i	pjat'-ь	krasiv-yx
we	saw	these-M.NOM.PL	five-NOM	beautiful-GEN.PL

lamp-ь.
table-GEN.PL (F)
'We saw these five beautiful lamps.'

Some types of DPs, however, do show special ACC morphology in the same positions. The DPs that display distinct accusative forms belong to one of three categories: (1) feminine singular, (2) animate, or (3) pronominal. Only a terminal element of a DP that falls into one of these three categories will ever show an accusative form distinct from the nominative. Consequently, we must regard membership in one of these three categories as a prerequisite for receiving VACC morphology from V.

This conclusion means that FA does not *always* apply when two elements merge, a possibility not countenanced by the formulation of FA in (28). I therefore restate FA in (76), to allow for such restrictions; and I stipulate the conditions (for Russian) under which VACC is assigned in (77).

(76) **Feature Assignment (FA), version 3 of 6**

    a. *Copying:* When α merges with β, forming [$_α$ α β], if α has satisfied its complementation requirements *and is designated as a feature assigner for β*, its grammatical features are immediately copied onto β ...

    b. *Realization:* ... and are realized as morphology on all lexical items dominated by β.

(77) **Russian-specific restriction on assignment of VACC**

V assigns VACC to β under FA only if

a. β is [+FEMININE] and not [−SINGULAR], or

b. β is [+ANIMATE], or

c. β is [+PRONOMINAL].

As noted above, it is the heterogeneous pattern of paucal and QUANT constructions as complements to V that shows that ACC is not assigned at all to direct objects that fail to meet the criteria in (77). That is why (once again, against tradition) I am arguing that these nominals are syntactically nominative—not accusative-marked nominals whose forms are merely syncretic with nominatives.

All things being equal, we expect quite a different pattern with paucal and QUANT nominals that do meet the criteria in (77) and do bear genuine ACC morphology. As we will see, this expectation is easily confirmed for paucal constructions. To see that it is also confirmed for QUANT constructions (which at first glance appear to disconfirm the prediction), however, will require a short digression into a topic that this monograph has mostly succeeded in avoiding: the actual *morphological realization* of VACC.

As is true throughout the Russian case system, the form taken by VACC morphology when applied to a particular nominal base depends on the declension class to which the noun in question belongs. Recall that most Russian nouns fall into one of three major declension classes, and that a noun's grammatical gender is mostly predictable from its declension class and its value for the feature [±HUMAN]. Other elements in the noun phrase, such as adjectives, demonstratives, and agreeing quantifiers, receive their gender as a consequence of agreement in the syntax.

The declension class of these elements is completely predictable from gender. In accordance with the findings reported by Halle and Matushansky (2006), I will assume that agreeing elements within the nominal phrase belong to two of the same declension classes relevant to nouns, despite superficial appearances, according to the following rules:

(78) **Rules for the assignment of declension class to agreeing elements (adjectives, demonstratives, etc.)**

a. [+FEMININE] → class 2

b. Otherwise → class 1

Declension class distinctions are suppressed in plural forms (not just plural forms of VACC). I will assume that this suppression of declension class distinctions is the result of a rule that assigns all bases to class 1 in the presence of a plural case suffix, regardless of the declension class membership of the corresponding singular.

(79) **Declension class assignment to [–SINGULAR] words (i.e.,
suppression of declension class distinctions in the plural)**
base → class 1 / __ [suffix, –SINGULAR]

Rule (79) is fed by rule (34) (repeated here for convenience), which determines the number of the case suffix in the first place—on the basis of the NBR value of the base, if it has one, and the NBR value of the feature assigned under FA otherwise.

(34) **How the NBR specification of case morphology is determined
(precedes rule (79))**
Morphology assigned by α to β under FA reflects
a. the NBR value of β if β is valued for NBR, and
b. the NBR value of α otherwise.

The rules by which Vᴀᴄᴄ is *realized* can now be stated for our purposes as in (80).[2]

(80) **Rules for realization of Vᴀᴄᴄ**
a. Vᴀᴄᴄ is realized as *-uju* (adjectives) or *-u* (other elements) / class 2 __
b. Vᴀᴄᴄ is syncretic with NGEN / class 1 __
c. Otherwise, Vᴀᴄᴄ is not realized.[3]

These realization rules will come into play, of course, only when Vᴀᴄᴄ has been assigned in the first place, in conformity with (77). This means (ignoring personal pronouns) that they will have an effect only within a DP that is either feminine singular or animate.

In this connection, it is important to bear in mind the crucial difference between two situations in which a complement DP may contain nominative forms: (1) the DP completely fails to receive Vᴀᴄᴄ because it falls under the criteria in (77); and (2) the DP receives Vᴀᴄᴄ but fails to realize it morphologically on one (or more) of its lexical items, because that lexical item falls under (80c). This distinction is not an artifact of the analysis, but corresponds to an irreducible difference in the facts that the analysis explains:

• In a situation of type 1, the entire DP "looks like a nominative DP," because it *is* a nominative DP. This is what we saw in (75).

• In a situation of type 2, only those lexical items within the DP that fall under (80c) will "look nominative." All other items in the same DP will "look accusative," bearing the morphology specified in (80a–b). This is what we see in (81) and (82)—most illuminatingly in (81b) and (82d), where the noun within DP "looks nominative" because it falls under (80c), but the rest of the lexical items "look accusative" because they do not fall under (80c).

(81) **DP complements to V that are assigned V$_{ACC}$ under (77a) (feminine singular DPs)**

    a. *Noun is class 2; falling under (80a)*
       Modifiers are feminine, hence class 2 by (78a); falling under (80a)

My	videli	èt-u	krasiv-uju	lamp-u.
we	saw	this-F.ACC.SG	beautiful-F.ACC.SG	lamp-ACC.SG (F)

       'We saw this beautiful lamp.'

    b. *Noun is class 3; falling under (80c)*
       Modifiers are feminine, hence class 2 by (78a); falling under (80a)

My	videli	èt-u	krasiv-uju
we	saw	this-F.ACC.SG	beautiful-F.ACC.SG

       tetrad'-ь.
       notebook-ACC.SG (F)[4]
       'We saw this beautiful notebook.'

(82) **DP complements to V that are assigned V$_{ACC}$ under (77b) (animate DPs)**

    a. *Noun is class 1(hence masculine) and singular; falling under (80b)*
       Modifiers are masculine singular, hence class 1 by (78b); falling under (80b)

My	videli	èt-ogo	molod-ogo
we	saw	this-M.ACC=GEN.SG	young-M.ACC=GEN.SG

       otc-a.
       father-ACC=GEN.SG (M)
       'We saw this young father.'

    b. *Noun is class 2, feminine, and singular (redundantly assigned V$_{ACC}$ under (77a))*
       Modifiers are feminine, hence class 2 by (78a); falling under (80a)

My	videli	èt-u	molod-uju	ženščin-u.
we	saw	this-F.ACC.SG	young-F.ACC.SG	woman-ACC (F)

       'We saw this young woman.'

    c. *Noun is class 2, masculine, and singular; falling under (80a)*
       Modifiers are masculine singular, hence class 1 by (78b); falling under (80b)

My	videli	èt-ogo	molod-ogo
we	saw	this-M.ACC=GEN.SG	young-M.ACC=GEN.SG

       mužčin-u.
       man-ACC.SG (M)
       'We saw this young man.'

d. *Noun is class 3 (hence feminine) and singular; falling under (80c)*
Modifiers are feminine, hence class 2 by (78a); falling under (80a)

My	videli	èt-u	molod-uju	mat'-ь.
we	saw	this-F.ACC.SG	young-F.ACC.SG	mother-ACC (F)

'We saw this young mother.'

e. *Noun is plural, hence class 1 by (79) regardless of class in*
singular; falling under (80b)
Modifiers are plural, hence class 1 by (79) regardless of class in
singular; falling under (80b)

My	videli	èt-ix	molod-yx
we	saw	this-ACC=GEN.PL	young-ACC=GEN.PL

otc-ov/ženščin-ь/mužčin-ь/mater-ej.
father/woman/man/mother-ACC=GEN.PL

'We saw these young fathers/women/men/mothers.'

As noted above, when Vᴀᴄᴄ is assigned to a paucal nominal that satisfies the criteria for Vᴀᴄᴄ assignment, the result is exactly as predicted. The pattern of number morphology is exactly the same as that found in nominals assigned Pᴏʙʟ, such as those in (31) and (32): the homogeneous pattern. The number-less noun shows plural morphology, just like agreement elements such as demonstratives and adjectives, as (83) illustrates.

(83) **DP complements to V that are assigned Vᴀᴄᴄ under (77b) (animate DPs) [continued]**
Paucal constructions
Noun is plural, hence class 1 by (79) regardless of class in singular;
falling under (80b)
Paucal Nʙʀ is plural, hence class 1 by (79) regardless of class in
singular; falling under (80b)
Modifiers are plural, hence class 1 by (79) regardless of class in
singular; falling under (80b)

My	videli	dv-ux	molod-yx
we	saw	two-ACC=GEN	young-ACC=GEN.PL

otc-ov/ženščin-ь/mužčin-ь/mater-ej.
father/woman/man/mother-ACC=GEN.PL

'We saw two young fathers/women/men/mothers.'

The explanation that applies to the identical pattern in oblique nominals applies here as well. V, like P, bears an unvalued, uninterpretable number feature, which probes and receives its value from the closest bearer of valued Nʙʀ as a consequence of the operation Agree. Vᴀᴄᴄ is only assigned in the first place to a paucal nominal if it is animate, given the conditions in (77), as

(75c) demonstrated. (Since a paucal DP is plural, (77a) does not apply—so feminine gender by itself will not trigger assignment of VACC to a paucal construction.) The presence of plural morphology on the noun in (83) also makes it clear that the morphology identical to the genitive here is *not* the "primeval NGEN," but morphology that has been assigned under FA.[5] The fact that the form of this morphology is identical to the genitive must result from true VACC/NGEN syncretism.

Once again, there is a crucial (and striking) contrast between the morphology of paucal nominals like the one in (83) that have been assigned VACC and the morphology of complement paucal nominals that are not assigned VACC at all. "Situation 1" paucal nominals like the one in (75c) that do not receive VACC show the heterogeneous pattern of case and number mismatches characteristic of nominative DPs because they *are* nominative DPs. "Situation 2" paucal nominals like the one in (83) show the homogeneous pattern expected of nominals whose heterogeneous DP-internal morphology has been overwritten by an external morphology-assigner, because their morphology has indeed been overwritten—by V assigning VACC. These nominals show the homogeneous pattern expected of accusative DPs because they (in contrast to nominals like the one in (75c)) *are* accusative DPs.

The trickiest point in the analysis of the Russian accusative comes when we consider how VACC applies to QUANT constructions with a nonpaucal numeral such as *pjat'* or a quantifier such as *mnogo* 'many'. As observed in chapter 6, note 2, many of these elements are morphologically exceptional in taking singular case suffixes, despite being grammatically plural.[6] For this reason, they do not trigger the declension-class-assigning rule in (79) when case suffixes are added, but retain their lexical declension class. If such a word does not lexically belong to class 1 or 2 already (and in fact, none do), it will fall under the "elsewhere" VACC realization rule (80c) and will fail to realize VACC morphology—even inside a DP that has been assigned VACC, as evidenced by the fact that other elements besides QUANT realize VACC within the DP. This is exactly what happens with the nonpaucal numerals and some other QUANT elements that move to D.[7] The forms *pjat'* and *mnogo* in (84) are identical to the nominative singular—not because FA failed to assign VACC, but because they fall under (80c) and therefore fail to realize the case that is assigned to them. The morphology on the noun and adjective, by contrast, does realize VACC (and is syncretic with the genitive, as required by (80b)).[8]

(84) **DP complements to V that are assigned Vacc under (77b) (animate DPs) (continued)**
Nonpaucal numeral constructions
Noun is plural, hence class 1 by (79) regardless of class in singular; falling under (80b)
Modifiers are plural, hence class 1 by (79) regardless of class in singular; falling under (80b)
Numeral is class 3 and exceptionally receives singular case Morphology; falling under (80c)

My	videli	pjat'/mnogo	molod-yx
we	saw	five/many	young-ACC=GEN.PL

otc-ov/ženščin-ъ/mužčin-ъ/mater-ej.
father/woman/man/mother-ACC=GEN.PL
'We saw five/many young fathers/women/men/mothers.'

7.2 Vergnaud-Licensing, "Default Nominative," and the Case of Subjects

I have proposed that Vacc morphology on the elements of a DP is a consequence of the DP's merger with a projection of V. When this merger takes place, if the requirements in (77) are also met, FA applies, with the morphological consequences discussed above. As argued in Pesetsky 1982, the same rule by which V assigns Vacc to its direct object is probably responsible for the Vacc morphology on duration phrases like the bracketed phrase in (85), which has also arguably merged with a projection of V.

(85) **Duration phrase assigned Vacc by V′**

My	peli	èt-u	pesnj-u	[vsj-u	nedelj-u].
we	sang	this-F.ACC.SG	song-ACC.SG	all-F.ACC.SG	week-ACC.SG

Examples like these suggest that this monograph is correct in offering a purely structural account of the distribution of accusative morphology. It is sisterhood to a projection of V that matters, not bearing a particular grammatical relation or θ-role.

On the other hand, not every DP that satisfies (77) and merges with V ends up bearing Vacc. In an unaccusative or passive construction in Russian, as in many other languages, the DP that initially merges with V typically bears Dnom morphology at the end of the derivation, rather than Vacc (see, e.g., Chvany 1975; Pesetsky 1982; Moore and Perlmutter 2000).

(86) **Dnom**

    a. *Passive*

       [Èt-a   krasiv-aja   lamp-a]   byl-a

       this-F.NOM.SG   beautiful-F.NOM.SG   lamp-NOM.SG   was-F.SG

       kuplen-a   včera.

       bought-F.SG   yesterday

       'This beautiful lamp was bought yesterday.'

    b. *Unaccusative*

       Bol'š-aja   rek-a   rastajal-a.

       big-F.NOM.SG   river-NOM.SG   melted-F.SG

       'The big river melted.'

The nominative DP in these constructions has a full array of properties otherwise associated exclusively with subjects in Russian (such as the ability to bind a reflexive pronoun and to control the subject of a verbal adverb clause). Such facts suggest that after initially merging with V, the DP remerges as a specifier of T (just as it does in languages like English).

It has always been tempting to link the subject properties of such nominals to their nominative case marking. That is why it is commonly proposed that nominative case is assigned to the underlying object by the same head that attracts it into subject position—namely, by T. In this monograph, however, I have argued for a very different view of nominative morphology. Though I have sometimes made informal reference to the notion "nominative environment," we have never needed to assume that nominative morphology is assigned to the elements of DP by anything other than D itself. Nothing external to the DP has played any role in the assignment of nominative morphology. Recall, for example, the logic of the proposed explanation for the fact that a direct object DP failing to meet the requirements for Vacc assignment by V in (77) bears nominative morphology. Nominative morphology appears on such a DP, not because some external element has assigned it, but because no external assigner of distinct morphology has erased it.

An explanation with the same logic might be offered for passive and unaccusative examples like (86a–b) as well. That is, we might propose that although the DPs in these examples seem to meet the requirements for Vacc assignment in their initial position, FA is blocked from applying to them there—and after they move, finite T assigns no morphology to them either. Here, too, the appearance of Dnom on the lexical items of a DP would once again be attributed to the absence of overwriting by other morphology, not to the presence of a DP-external Dnom assigner.

To what might we attribute the failure of Vᴀᴄᴄ assignment to the underlying complement of a passive or unaccusative verb? The answer must lie in some property that distinguishes such verbs from their active, non-unaccusative counterparts. An obvious candidate is their inability to satisfy the special licensing requirement for DPs first posited by Vergnaud (2006 [orig. 1976]). Though Vergnaud and his successors called this requirement *Case*, I will call it *Vergnaud-licensing*, to avoid confusion. As Burzio (1981, 1986), Chomsky (1981, chap. 2), and others observed in the wake of Vergnaud's proposal, if the direct object position in an unaccusative or passive VP is not a position of Vergnaud-licensing, but a position such as the specifier of finite T is, the obligatory raising of the DP complement to passive and unaccusative verbs could be explained.

Vergnaud-licensing was called "Case" (and the licensing requirement, the "Case Filter"), because of the similarity between the repertoire of Vergnaud-licensing positions and the set of positions that license the various types of case morphology in languages like Latin. In the context of this monograph, however, examples like (86a–b) suggest that the link between case morphology and licensing is actually limited to the principle in (87).

(87) **FA and licensing**
   FA applies to DP only in the position in which it is Vergnaud-licensed.

Given (87), if the case morphology on a DP reflects an external assigner at all, it reflects the assigner available in the position where that DP is Vergnaud-licensed.[9] Whenever a DP merges in a Vergnaud-licensing position where FA fails to apply, however, and whenever a DP merges in a *non*-Vergnaud-licensing position where FA might otherwise have applied, the lexical items of that DP will bear morphology that does not reflect an external assigner: the Dɴᴏᴍ morphology that they received from D.[10]

Though we have arrived at this conclusion as a result of the proposals made here concerning Nɢᴇɴ and the morphosyntax of Russian, the conclusion itself is far from new. It amounts to the claim that nominative case in Russian is a *default*, in precisely the sense enunciated and explored by Schütze (1997, 2001; see also Pereltsvaig 2007a, 106–111, for Russian). Schütze argues that nominative case in languages such as German and Icelandic is a strictly morphological default, assigned to the elements of a nominal when no other case morphology has been assigned. At the same time, however, he stresses that "licensing and morphological case are independent systems. ... [D]efault case in my sense can never 'save' a DP from violating the Case Filter" (Schütze 2001, 206). Schütze's arguments and conclusions converge with mine.

Furthermore, although Russian finite T does not assign its features under FA, in contrast to D, N, V, and P (with the consequence that what appears on the subject of a finite clause is "default" DNOM), T might be a morphology assigner in other languages. For example, although the English pronominal series traditionally called "accusative" (*me, him, her,* etc.) appears to be a default, as Schütze argues, the pronominal series traditionally called "nominative" (*I, he, she,* etc.) might reflect the assignment of morphology under FA by T. This might explain why the "nominative" forms are used in spoken English only for pronouns that are merged with T, and not in the many other environments where languages like Russian and Latin show DNOM morphology, such as the focus of a cleft (*It is me who* ...), conjunction (*Sue and me are* ...), and so on.

Even in Russian, where finite T does not assign morphology to elements such as its specifier, it is possible that certain types of *nonfinite* T do assign morphology. If some infinitival TPs can be analyzed as headed by a null counterpart to the English infinitival marker *to,* and if the subject position of such an infinitival is a Vergnaud-licensing environment, it would come as no surprise to find constructions in which PDAT is assigned to the subject of such an infinitive. Moore and Perlmutter (2000) argue that the subjects in examples like (88) instantiate just this possibility, in contrast to other apparent preverbal dative subjects, which they analyze as scrambled indirect objects (but see Fleisher 2006 for an alternative biclausal analysis that does not posit dative subjects).

(88) **Dative subject of infinitive: Assigned by null *to*?**
    [Èt-omu   student-u]   ne   sda-t'
     this-M.DAT.SG   student-DAT.SG   NEG   pass-INF
    èkzamen.
    examination-NOM (trad. ACC)
    'It's not (in the cards) for this student to pass the exam.'
    (expanded from Moore and Perlmutter 2000, 387 ex. (24a))

Note finally that (87) does not prevent Ā-movement or scrambling from applying to a DP that has received morphology under FA, and retaining this morphology after movement. For example, VACC morphology is preserved under *wh*-movement.

(89) **VACC preserved under *wh*-movement**
    Kak-uju   lamp-u   vy   videli?
    what.kind.of-F.ACC.SG   lamp-ACC.SG (F)   you   saw
    'What kind of lamp did you see?'

7.3   Prepositions That Appear to Assign VACC

VACC morphology is not limited to DP direct objects of main verbs; it is found on the nominal objects of a small class of prepositions as well. Though I will not have a full analysis of this fact to offer, it cannot be overlooked or swept under the rug—since the very existence of VACC on the object of a preposition might be taken as a challenge to this monograph's central claim: that syntactic categories and cases are one and the same. All things being equal, we do not expect to find a preposition assigning the morphology that has been declared the exclusive province of V.

We might conjecture, however, that VACC in these prepositional constructions actually is assigned by a null verb, which cooccurs with the visible preposition. Some evidence does in fact support the presence of an unseen head in these constructions. As is often observed (see, e.g., Timberlake 2004, 181–182), almost every "accusative-assigning" preposition in Russian has a second use in which its object bears some version of POBL. If we focus on the spatial uses of these prepositions, it turns out that the VACC variant denotes motion along a *path toward* the very same location that the POBL variant denotes *location in*, as illustrated in (90).[11]

(90) **POBL-VACC alternations among prepositions with spatial uses (feminine noun)**

Location

a. Ona žila [v malen'k-oj komnat-e].
    she lived in small-F.PREP.SG room-PREP
    'She lived in a small room.'

c. Miša sidel [na skamejk-e].
    Misha sat on bench-PREP
    'Misha was sitting on the bench.'

e. Ol'ga rabotaet [za granic-ej].
    Olga works beyond border-INSTR
    'Olga works abroad.'

g. Den'gi naxodjatsja [pod poduš k-oj].
    money is.located under pillow-INSTR
    'The money is located under the pillow.'

Direction

b. Ona pošla [v malen'k-uju komnat-u].
    she went in small-F.ACC.SG room-ACC
    'She went into a small room.'

d. Miša sel [na skamejk-u].
    Misha sat on bench-acc
    'Misha sat down on the bench.'

f. Ol'ga často ezdit [za granic-u].
    Olga often goes beyond border-ACC
    'Olga often travels abroad.'

h. On položil den'gi [pod poduš k-u].
    he put money under pillow-ACC
    'He put the money under the pillow.'

Similar phenomena have been extensively investigated in other Indo-European languages such as German. This research has concluded that the structure of a VACC spatial preposition construction is more complex than it seems, containing (at the very least) a directional head called DIR (or PATH), whose complement is a location-denoting phrase containing the kind of preposition that we expect to assign POBL (see Koopman 2000; Van Riemsdijk and Huybregts 2001, 2006; Cinque and Rizzi 2010). The semantic intuition behind these analyses is that of Jackendoff (1990, 45) and others who have suggested that an expression like *into the room* in *John went into the room* or (90b) is semantically decomposed as [$_{PATH}$ TO [$_{PLACE}$ IN [$_{THING}$ ROOM]]]. Though the higher DIR head may be silent in some languages (such as Russian), in others, such as the Caucasian language Lezgian, it is overt (Van Riemsdijk and Huybregts 2001, 2006; data from Haspelmath 1993).

Discussing the German counterparts to (90), Noonan (2010, 169) proposes that the element responsible for the case of the DP object of P in directional constructions is DIR itself, and that the case assigned by DIR is *accusative* because DIR belongs to the category V. (She calls this verb "abstract GO.") If we adopt her proposal for Russian as well, the presence of VACC morphology in the directional constructions of (90) no longer poses any special challenge to the central hypotheses of this monograph. All things being equal, VACC morphology is just what one expects to find on the terminal elements of a phrase that merges with a verb.

Crucially, the locational complement to DIR must be a DP and not a PP, as shown in (91); otherwise, wrong predictions are made about the case marking of certain nominals.

(91) **Structure of directional constructions**

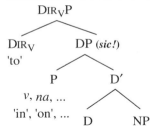

If the sister of DIR were headed by P rather than D as in (91), POBL morphology would be assigned to the nominal itself, just as it is in nondirectional PPs. Before DIR is merged, the nominals in the right-hand column of (90) would receive exactly the morphology that they bear in the left-hand column. Once DIR merges, if the nominal is feminine, animate, or pronominal (assuming P inherits those properties from the nominal, perhaps by Agree), POBL morphology will be overwritten by VACC, as provided by rule (77). This does yield the correct result for these cases.

The problem arises if the nominal is neither feminine, nor animate, nor pronominal—the circumstances under which rule (77) *refrains* from assigning VACC. For nominal direct objects, this proposal had the correct consequence that the morphology that survives on a masculine inanimate nonpronominal

DP is the morphology that was assigned most recently to it, namely, Dɴᴏᴍ. If the complement to Dɪʀ in (91) were a PP, however, the morphology assigned most recently would not be Dɴᴏᴍ, but Pᴏʙʟ. This is not what we find. A masculine inanimate DP in a directional phrase does not bear Pᴏʙʟ morphology; rather, it bears Dɴᴏᴍ, just as it does when it is the direct object of a verb.

(92) **Pᴏʙʟ-Dɴᴏᴍ alternations among prepositions with spatial uses (masculine inanimate noun)**

a. Ona	žila	[v malen'k-om	dom-e].
she	lived	in small-ᴍ.ᴘʀᴇᴘ.sɢ	house-ᴘʀᴇᴘ
'She lived in a small house.'			

b. Ona	pošla	[v malen'k-ij	dom-ъ].
she	went	in small-ᴍ.ɴᴏᴍ.sɢ	house-ɴᴏᴍ
'She went into a small house.'			

If the correct structure is (91), however, the correct predictions are made in such cases. If P is not the head of the phrase that contains it, it will not assign Pᴏʙʟ morphology to its sister in (91). Consequently, when Dɪʀ merges, the most recently assigned morphology on the elements of DP is Dɴᴏᴍ. Since Vᴀᴄᴄ is not assigned to a masculine inanimate object, it should continue to show Dɴᴏᴍ. As (92b) shows, this prediction is correct.

As we will see in chapter 8, an entirely different set of considerations leads to precisely the same conclusion, lending support to the structure in (91) and the proposed treatment of what looked like Vᴀᴄᴄ-assigning prepositions. Of course, it is now important to establish the principles that require the pattern of projection in (91), while restricting similar D-headed prepositional constructions in other environments. We do not find phrases elsewhere that look like PPs, but are transparent to case assignment from outside, like the DP in (91). What motivates the unusual choice of head in (91) is therefore a property of Dɪʀ that is unique to this construction: for example, a semantic requirement for a phrase that *names* a location, rather than supplying a locational argument for a predicate (as in the left-hand column of (90))—a distinction that might correlate with a DP/PP distinction. Though this is a significant loose end, I must leave it untied for now.

As noted by Timberlake (2004, 181–182), constructions that we would now analyze as instances of (91) have a number of idiomatic (i.e., apparently noncompositional) uses as well. For example, *pod*, which otherwise means 'under', is used with the accusative to denote an "adapted function" in examples like (93a), and *v* 'in' is used with the accusative to denote resemblance in examples like (93b).[12]

(93) **Idiomatic uses of (91)**

    a. Narkodel'cy   snjali   kvartiru   i   oborudovali   ee

       drug.dealers   rented   apartment   and   equipped   it

    pod   laboratorij-u.

    under   laboratory-ACC

    'The drug dealers rented an apartment and converted it into a

    laboratory.'

    (http://www.tatar-inform.ru/iphone/news/266298, accessed January 30,

    2012)

    b. Aleksej   byl   **v**   **batjušk-u.**

       Aleksej   was   **into**   **dad-ACC**

       'Aleksej took after (his) dad.'

       (Peškovskij 1928, 306; cited in Billings 1995, 25)

We might regard as similarly idiomatic the use of *v* 'in' with ACC (or NOM, for DPs that fail to satisfy (77)) in temporal expressions that situate an event on reference to time intervals smaller than a week, as seen in (94a–d), or vague in their boundaries, as seen in (94e).[13]

(94) **Temporal uses of (91)**

    Èto slučilos' …

    'This happened …

a. … v	sred-**u**.			b. … v		Pasx-**u**.
… into	Wednesday-**ACC**			… into		Easter-**ACC**
… on Wednesday.'				… on Easter.'		
c. … v	t-**u**	že	minut-**u**.	d. … v	tri	čas-a.
… into	that-**ACC**	same	minute-**ACC**	… into	three.NOM	hour-**GEN**
… at the very same moment.'				… at three o'clock.'		
e. … v	sovsem	drug-**uju**	èpox-**u**.			
… into	completely	different-**ACC**	epoch-**ACC**			
… in a completely different epoch.'						
(Nesset 2004, 6 ex. (9))						

In the absence of a predictive proposal from which these and other nonspatial uses of prepositions with accusative nominals follow, I leave them as a possible loose end.

In contrast to prepositions that fail to assign POBL because they do not project (upon merger with DP), Russian also appears to boast two prepositions that do project, but fail to assign POBL as a lexical property. Failure to assign morphology under FA is a property we have already seen for finite (as opposed to infinitival) T and for V with complements that fail to meet the Russian-specific criteria in (77).

The first case involves the (multitalented) preposition *v* in expressions of "assuming a role" (Mel'čuk 1985, 461–489; Pereltsvaig 2006; Corbett 2008).

In this construction, the object of the preposition is required to be plural (a fact that I will not explain) and bears nominative morphology, otherwise unknown for this preposition.[14]

(95) **Role-assuming use of *v* + nominative**

Putin	soglasen	ballotirovat'sja	v	prezident-y.
Putin.NOM	agree	to.run	*v*	president-NOM.PL

'Putin agrees to run for president.'
(Pereltsvaig 2006, 477 ex. (66))

The second case involves the distributive preposition *po*, which has a number of much-studied peculiarities (Franks 1995, 139ff.), including distinctive behavior with DPs containing paucals or numerals. When the complement of distributive *po* does *not* contain a paucal or numeral moved to D, it assigns Pᴅᴀᴛ, as seen in (96a–b). When its DP complement does contain a paucal or numeral in D, the DP is generally nominative, as seen in (96c–d).

(96) **Distributive *po* + nominative (animate masculine) DP in the presence of a paucal/ Qᴜᴀɴᴛ element**

Každaja devuška priglasila …

'Each girl invited…

No paucal or numeral: Pᴅᴀᴛ object

a. … po mal'čik-u.
… DISTR boy-DAT.SG
… a boy each.'

b. … po odn-omu mal'čik-u.
… DISTR one-DAT.SG boy-DAT.SG
… one boy each.'

Paucal or numeral: Dɴᴏᴍ object

c. … po dva mal'čik-a.
… DISTR two.NOM boy-GEN.SG°
… two boys each.'

d. … po pjat'-ь mal'čik-ov.
… DISTR five-NOM boy-GEN.PL
… five boys each.'

As Harves notes (2003, 246 n. 6; crediting Yakov Testelets, personal communication), a *po*-phrase of any description may not itself function as an object of a preposition, which not only provides an argument that we are dealing with a species of P in all the examples of (96), but also provides an argument that P, rather than D, projects in all these examples.

As a complement to V in (96), the *po*-phrases meet none of the criteria for assignment of Vᴀᴄᴄ in (77). As a consequence, if *po* idiosyncratically refrains from assigning Pᴅᴀᴛ in the presence of a paucal or numeral, its DP complement will look nominative and display the heterogeneous pattern of case (and number) marking familiar from nominative DPs. This is particularly striking when the DP complement to *po* is animate, paucal, and singular, as in (96c), or feminine and singular, as in (97), which coincidentally also contains an instance of "role-assuming *v*."

(97) **Distributive *po* + nominative feminine DP**

Každ-omu	dali	v	pomoščicy	[**po**	dv-**e**
each.one-DAT.SG	they.gave	*v*	assistants.FEM	*po*	two-**NOM**

sanitark-**i**].
nurse-**GEN.SG**°

'They gave each one two nurses as assistants.'
(adapted from Mel'čuk 1985, 448)

The heterogeneous (nominative-looking) DP morphology seen in (96c) and (97) is otherwise unknown in feminine or masculine animate singular nominals as complements of transitive verbs or prepositions (usually regarded as) assigning accusative case. It is exactly what we expect, however, if *po* is a preposition heading a PP that happens not to assign POBL—at least when its complement contains a paucal or numeral. Why *po* should behave differently when its complement fails to contain a paucal or numeral, however, remains a mystery.[15]

8   Argument 2 for the Core Proposal: "You Are What You Assign"

8.1   Feature Assignment and Adnominals

Though we have seen a number of arguments that Russian nouns are "born genitive" and acquire other types of case marking derivationally, we have not yet explored one of the most significant consequences of this proposal in any depth: the expectation that because N *is* genitive, it should also *assign* genitive. This chapter takes up this topic. In the course of investigating genitive assignment by N, we will also explore another topic missing from the discussion so far: the interaction of morphology assignment by FA with the laws that regulate how the syntax communicates with the phonology.

We have already appealed to assignment of NGEN by N as an explanation for the presence of NGEN morphology on adjectives in paucal and QUANT constructions like (1b) and (2). These adjectives receive NGEN from N (after merging with N′) for the same reason that demonstratives and adjectives that precede paucals and QUANT receive DNOM morphology from D (after merging with D′), as discussed in section 4.2. The same idea is also the most obvious explanation for the most prominent use of genitive case cross-linguistically: as a marker of *adnominal DPs*. These adnominal DPs are a semantically heterogeneous class that includes complements, possessors,[1] and the "genitive of quality" constructions explored by Nikolaeva (2007) and others. If the bracketed adnominal DPs in (98a–b) enter the derivation by merging with a projection of N, we may straightforwardly analyze their NGEN morphology as a consequence of FA. A category that merges with a projection of N is expected to receive NGEN morphology.

(98) **Adnominal genitive DPs (nominative environment)**
   a. *Possessor*
      krasivy-j   stol-ъ   [_DP_ molod-ogo
      beautiful-M.NOM.SG   table-NOM.SG   young-M.GEN.SG
      aktër-a]
      actor-GEN.SG
      'the young actor's beautiful table'
   b. *Complement*
      poln-oe   uničtoženi-e   [_DP_ bol'š-ogo
      complete-N.NOM.SG   destruction-NOM.SG   big-M.GEN.SG
      gorod-a]
      city-GEN.SG
      'the complete destruction of the big city'
   c. *Genitive of quality*
      roskošn-oe   kresl-o
      luxurious-N.NOM.SG   armchair-NOM.SG
      [_DP_ krasn-oj   plastmass-y]
         red-F.GEN.SG   plastic-GEN.SG
      'a luxurious armchair (made of) red plastic'
      (Nikolaeva 2007, 60 ex. (187))

We may also assume that they are Vergnaud-licensed (i.e., assigned what has traditionally been called abstract Case) within NP, either by N or by some higher functional element.

In the context of the present monograph, we should ask first, of course, whether the genitive morphology on the bracketed DPs in (98) really is assigned from outside the bracketed DP, or whether it might realize "primeval genitive" (perhaps because some hidden element moves to D within the adnominal). The behavior of paucal and QUANT elements, and especially the behavior of pre-D adjectives and demonstratives in genitive adnominals, makes it clear that this instance of genitive case truly is assigned from outside the DP. Every element in the DP, including the paucal or QUANT element, bears NGEN morphology here, which we expect only if the source of NGEN morphology is an assigner external to DP. I return below to the plural number morphology on N and on the postpaucal adjective in (99a).

(99) **Paucal adnominal genitive DPs (nominative environment)**

   a. krasivy-j   stol-ъ   [$_{DP}$ èt-ix
      beautiful-M.NOM.SG   table-NOM.SG   these-GEN.PL
      posledn-ix   dvu-x   molod-yx   aktër-ov]
      last-GEN.PL   DUAL-GEN   young-GEN.PL actor-GEN.PL
      'these last two young actors' beautiful table'

   b. poln-oe   uničtoženi-e   [$_{DP}$ èt-ix
      complete-N.NOM.SG   destruction-NOM.SG   these-GEN.PL
      posledn-ix   pjat-i   bol'š-ix   gorod-ov]
      last-GEN.PL   five-GEN   big-GEN.PL   city-GEN.PL
      'the complete destruction of these last five big cities'

   c. malen'k-ij   rebënok-ъ   [$_{DP}$ dvu-x   let-ъ]^2
      small-M.NOM.SG   child-NOM.SG   two-GEN   year-GEN.PL
      'a small child of two years' (i.e., 'two years old')

In the theory of case advanced in this monograph, the assignment of genitive to adnominals is just the flip side of the fact that N itself is born genitive. The morphology of adnominals in examples like (98) and (99) thus appears to provide crucial evidence for the overall proposal.[3]

8.2 An Apparent Locality Restriction on Feature Assignment

Nonetheless, there is a serious problem with the analysis in its present form. I have argued that nominal phrases in Russian are DPs. This means that the nominal phrases in (98) and (99) that embed the bracketed DPs are themselves NPs, merged as complements to D. None of these examples contains any QUANT element that needs to move to D. Consequently, the theory so far incorrectly predicts that this D should assign D$_{NOM}$ morphology to *all* the terminal elements of its complement. Though this prediction might appear correct for the head nouns *stol* 'table' and *uničtoženie* 'destruction' and the adjectives that modify them, it is wildly incorrect for the adnominal possessive DP in (98a) and (99a) and the complement DP in (98b) and (99b)—or else we would never have had the chance to observe the adnominal genitive morphology that has been the topic of this section so far. Instead, the result should have been uniform D$_{NOM}$ morphology, that is, the homogeneous patterns in (100).

(100) **False prediction for adnominal DPs (nominative environment)**

a. *[_{DP} D [_{NP} krasivy-j   stol-ъ   [_{DP} molod-oj
                        beautiful-NOM.SG   table-NOM.SG   young-NOM.SG

aktër-ъ]]]
actor-NOM.SG

b. *[_{DP} D [_{NP} poln-oe   uničtoženi-e
                        complete-NOM.SG   destruction-NOM.SG

[_{DP} bol'š-oj   gorod-ъ]]]
    big-NOM.SG   city-NOM.SG

What prevents the higher D from placing D_{NOM} morphology on the terminal elements of the embedded adnominal in (98)–(99)? The problem is in fact much more general. Not only the higher D, but *every* element merged later than this D is unable to assign morphology into the bracketed adnominal. For example, if a preposition that assigns P_{OBL} morphology is merged with the DPs in (98) or (99), it will deposit dative morphology on the head noun and other elements within the higher DP—but once again, the terminal elements of the adnominal DP remain untouched and genitive, as (101) and (102) show.

(101) **Adnominal genitive DPs (oblique environment)**

a. [_{PP} (k)   [_{DP} D [_{NP} krasiv-omu   stol-u
        (to)   beautiful-DAT.SG   table-DAT.SG

[_{DP} molod-**ogo**   aktër-**a**]]]]
    young-**GEN**.SG   actor-**GEN**.SG
    'to the young actor's beautiful table'

b. [_{PP} (k)   [_{DP} D [_{NP} poln-omu   uničtoženij-u
        (to)   complete-DAT.SG   destruction-DAT.SG

[_{DP} bol'š-**ogo**   gorod-**a**]]]]
    big-**GEN**.SG   city-**GEN**.SG
    'to the complete destruction of the big city'

(102) **False prediction for adnominal DPs (oblique environment)**

a. *[_{PP} (k)   [_{DP} D [_{NP} krasiv-omu   stol-u
        (to)   beautiful-DAT.SG   table-DAT.SG

[_{DP} molod-**omu**   aktër-**u**]]]]
    young-**DAT**.SG   actor-**DAT**.SG

b. *[_{PP} (k)   [_{DP} D [_{NP} poln-omu   uničtoženij-u
        (to)   complete-DAT.SG   destruction-DAT.SG

[_{DP} bol'š-**omu**   gorod-**u**]]]]
    big-**DAT**.SG   city-**DAT**.SG

The same problem arises if a verb is substituted for the preposition. If a DP like those under discussion merges with V, and the DP has the right properties to receive VACC from the verb (as discussed in the preceding section), the proposal predicts incorrectly that the terminal elements of the adnominal DP should show VACC morphology. In reality, though the rest of the nominal does receive VACC morphology, the adnominal itself once again remains genitive.

(103) **Adnominal genitive DPs (accusative environment)**
My   videli   [$_{DP}$ D [$_{NP}$ krasiv-uju   lamp-u
we   saw   beautiful-F.ACC.SG   lamp-ACC.SG
[$_{DP}$ molod-oj   aktris-y]]].
    young-GEN.SG   actress-GEN.SG
    'We saw the young actress's beautiful lamp.'

(104) **False prediction for adnominal DPs (accusative environment)**
*My   videli   [$_{DP}$ D [$_{NP}$ krasiv-uju   lamp-u
we   saw   beautiful-F.ACC.SG   lamp-ACC.SG
[$_{DP}$ molod-uju   aktris-u]]].
    young-ACC.SG   actress-ACC.SG

It looks as though feature assignment to the terminal elements of an adnominal DP is being blocked when its source is any element other than the N (or projection of N) with which the adnominal DP was merged. This observation is schematized in (105).

(105) *α's morphology may not end up on β*

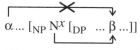

α... [$_{NP}$ N^x [$_{DP}$ ... β ...]]

N's morphology may end up on β

The problem is even more widespread. Consider a configuration that is the inverse of (105), with N^x and α switching places. If N or a projection of N attempts to assign NGEN to a DP that did not merge with it, but is instead *contained within* a phrase that merged with it, it is now NGEN assignment by N^x that fails, as schematized in (106).

(106) *N's morphology may not end up on β*

N^x ... [$_{αP}$ α [$_{DP}$ ... β ...]]

α's morphology may end up on β

The noun *ljubov'* 'love', for example, takes a PP complement (bearing the θ-role "target of emotion") headed by the PDAT-assigning preposition *k* 'to, for'. The terminal elements of the DP complement to P in this configuration bear the P_{DAT} morphology that *k* assigns. Crucially, this morphology is not overwritten by N_{GEN} assigned by N, as should happen under the theory so far.

(107) **Adnominal complement PP containing a DP (nominative environment)**
[ljubov'-ь [_{PP} k [_{DP} D [_{NP} trë-m   apel'sin-am]]]]
love-NOM for   three-DAT   orange-DAT.PL
'love for three oranges'

(108) **False prediction for adnominal complement PP containing a DP (nominative environment)**
*[ljubov'-ь [_{PP} k [_{DP} D [_{NP} trë-x   apel'sin-ov]]]]
love-NOM for   three-GEN   orange-GEN.PL
'love for three oranges'

The same noun may also take a noncomplement DP adnominal (bearing the θ-role "experiencer"), which omits the preposition. Under these circumstances and these circumstances alone, N_{GEN} appears on the terminal elements of the adnominal noncomplement.

(109) **Adnominal DP (nominative environment)**
[ljubov'-ь [_{DP} D [_{NP} trë-x   apel'sin-ov]]]
love-NOM   three-GEN   orange-GEN.PL
'love of (i.e., on the part of) three oranges'

It looks as though we are dealing with a locality restriction on FA—but of what sort? The problem is clearly not a general prohibition on assigning morphology across a maximal projection. Throughout our discussion, we have seen many examples in which morphology is assigned across such a boundary (e.g., the assignment of D_{NOM} to elements of NP and the assignment of P_{OBL} or V_{ACC} to the elements of DP). Nor is the problem as simple as a prohibition against assignment across *multiple* maximal projections, since we have seen many examples of this as well. For instance, when assignment by P deposits P_{OBL} case morphology on the elements of an NP, it crosses both a DP and an NP boundary to do so. The same happens when V places V_{ACC} morphology on the elements of NP within its DP complement.

Instead, the problem appears to be specific to assignment across a *DP* boundary. Here too, however, we cannot exclude assignment across DP in general, since we have also seen many examples in which P, V—and now N—deposit morphology on the terminal elements of DPs that merge with them. Instead, what (105) and (106) suggest is that assignment across a DP boundary is restricted to the element with which that DP merged, as schematized in (110).

(110) *γ's morphology may not end up on β*

$$\gamma \ldots [_{\alpha P} \ \alpha \, [_{DP} \ \ldots \ \beta \ldots]]$$

α's morphology may end up on β

8.3 Explanation for the Locality Restriction

DPs have, of course, been argued to be special in another context: they belong to the subset of constituents called *phases*. The construction of a phase by iterated, recursive Merge has been argued to trigger the operation *Spell-Out*, which transmits information about the syntactic derivation to the phonological components of the grammar. Though there are different proposals about the kinds of information that are transmitted and about the impact of Spell-Out on the syntax itself (Chomsky 2001, 2004; Matushansky 2005; Fox and Pesetsky 2005), constant across the various proposals is the idea that Spell-Out of a phase tells the phonology what syntactic units it needs to pronounce, and how they should be linearized. This information may be supplemented as the result of later instances of Spell-Out, but may not be erased. The relation between the syntactic and phonological derivations is monotonic.

Assume that Spell-Out of a phase Φ tells the phonology, among other things, what morphemes are present on the lexical items contained within Φ. (Realization rules like those for V$_{ACC}$ in (80) might apply in the phonology, taking as input the information received from the syntax as the result of Spell-Out.) If this is so, then no instance of FA that applies *after* the Spell-Out of Φ will ever have a detectable effect on the pronunciation of the terminal elements of Φ. The lexical items of Φ will be forever frozen in the form that they had already taken at the moment of Spell-Out. The presence of genitive morphology on the terminal elements of the adnominals in the problematic unstarred examples discussed in this chapter—despite the presence of higher elements that should have deposited their features in the form of morphology on these terminal elements—may then be taken as examples of the freezing effect of Spell-Out on the pronunciation of the adnominal DP.

What becomes crucial is the timing of Spell-Out: when precisely is a phase spelled out? The observation in (110) appears to teach us that Spell-Out of a phase Φ is triggered only after Φ has undergone Merge, and that FA applies immediately *before* Spell-Out, as outlined in (111).

(111) **Timing of operations relevant to Spell-Out of a phase Φ**

Step 1: The syntax constructs Φ.

Step 2: Merge (α, Φ).

Step 3: FA applies.

Step 4: Spell-Out applies to Φ (freezing it for further applications
of FA).

For the sake of clarity, we might also revise FA as follows, where "accessible" means 'not contained within a previously spelled-out domain'.

(112) **Feature Assignment (FA), version 4 of 6**

a. ***Copying:*** When α merges with β, forming [α α β], if α has
satisfied its complementation requirements and is designated as a
feature assigner for β, its grammatical features are immediately
copied
onto β…

b. ***Realization:*** … and are realized as morphology on all *accessible*
lexical items dominated by β.

This emendation in (112) is unnecessary if one is willing to posit applications of FA across phase boundaries that remain undetectable because they no longer influence the phonology (and nothing else interacts with the morphology assigned under FA). The emendation is also unnecessary if spelling out of a constituent renders the lexical items that it dominates invisible to subsequent processes, as theories of phases like Chomsky's entail (but not others; e.g., Fox and Pesetsky 2005). Since the emendation is empirically harmless, I will assume it as stated in what follows.

If this proposal is tenable, we solve the problems considered in this chapter. When an adnominal DP merges with N, FA applies immediately, assigning NGEN morphology to the elements of the adnominal DP. The next step in the derivation spells out the adnominal DP. From this point on, its terminals will retain the NGEN morphology that they bore at the moment of Spell-Out. Likewise, in (107), merger of the preposition *k* with its object DP was followed by assignment of PDAT to the terminal elements of DP, an operation that in turn was immediately followed by Spell-Out of that DP. As a consequence, when the PP headed by *k* is merged as a complement of N, NGEN does not show up on the DP object of the preposition, since the pronunciation of the contents of this DP are frozen in the form they took at the moment of Spell-Out.

This result, if correct, provides the promised second reason for positing the D-headed prepositional construction in (91) that was crucial to our analysis of prepositions that (seem to) assign VACC. If the complement to DIR were a PP (rather than the preposition-containing DP motivated by the morphological facts), DIR would not be able to assign VACC across PP to the nominal. DIR would be an instance of γ in (110), and the PP would be an instance of αP, blocking FA by DIR to β, the nominal. If the complement is a DP, DIR is α and the DP is β, posing no obstacle to the assignment of VACC to the nominal.

Finally, small clause constructions suggest that Spell-Out, like FA, also applies to DP only once it is Vergnaud-licensed. If the bracketed DP in (113) enters the derivation as the subject of a small clause whose predicate is the adjective 'beautiful', Spell-Out of this DP must be delayed until the higher verb is merged; otherwise, we expect to find its lexical items marked with DNOM morphology, not the VACC morphology that actually appears.

(113) **Small clause construction**

    Ja   sčitaju   [èt-u   lamp-u]   krasiv-oj.

    I   consider   this-F.ACC.SG lamp-ACC.SG beautiful-F.INSTR.SG[4]

    'I consider this lamp beautiful.'

Suppose the subject of a small clause must raise into the higher VP in order to be Vergnaud-licensed (as argued for English Exceptional Case Marking constructions by Chomsky (2008), adapting proposals by Postal (1974) and by Lasnik and Saito (1991)). If a DP undergoes Spell-Out only once it is Vergnaud-licensed, the presence of VACC on *ètu lampu* in (113), rather than DNOM, is accounted for. The bracketed DP does not undergo Spell-Out until after it remerges with a projection of the higher verb, which assigns VACC to it.

If the speculations offered at the end of section 7.2 concerning the morphology of subject pronouns and infinitival subjects prove correct, they provide further arguments for the same point: FA affects a DP after it moves for reasons of Vergnaud-licensing.

8.4   Stress Shifts in Numberless Nouns

With much of our analysis of adnominal genitive case assignment now in place, we are in a position to discuss a phonological peculiarity of paucal constructions that has often been taken as crucial evidence in favor of approaches to such constructions quite different from the one developed in this monograph. We have claimed that the case morphology on a noun in a nominative paucal construction is the same as that found on the noun of an adnominal DP: namely, NGEN. Famously, however, five Russian nouns of declension class 1 show a difference in word stress between these two environments: *rjad* 'row', *čas* 'hour', *šar* 'sphere', *šag* 'step', and *sled* 'trace'. Though the segmental content of the case suffix is the same (-*a*), stress falls on the stem in an adnominal genitive DP, but on the suffix in a nominative paucal construction.

(114) a. **Adnominal nonpaucal DP with a noun of the *rjad* group (nominative environment)**
       Stem stress

konec-ъ	[_DP èt-ogo	posledn-ego	rj**á**d-a]
end-NOM.SG	this-NOM.SG	last-GEN.SG	row-GEN.SG

'the end of this last row'

   b. **Paucal DP with a noun of the *rjad* group (nominative environment)**
      Suffix stress

èt-i	posledn-ie	dva	rjad-**á**
these-NOM.PL	last-NOM.PL	DUAL.NOM	row-GEN.NUMBERLESS

'these last two rows'

Though the suffix found in a nominative paucal environment on the five nouns of this class is segmentally identical to the normal NGEN suffix -*a*, as can be seen in (114a–b), this difference in stress has been taken by some researchers as evidence that the case of a noun in a nominative paucal construction is not genitive at all—in sharp contrast to the proposal advanced here. Some of these researchers posit a special case assigned by the paucal numerals (Isačenko 1962, 529–530, as cited in Mel'čuk 1985, 174; Zaliznjak 1967, 46–48; Rappaport 2002, 2003b; see also Franks 1994, 600 n. 3), called the *sčëtnaja forma* 'numerative form' by Isačenko and Zaliznjak and *paucal case* by Rappaport. Others suggest that the inflection found on nouns in nominative paucal constructions is actually the *nominative* form of a special *paucal number* on nouns, and that what looks like genitive plural morphology on modifying elements is actually the nominative-case, paucal-number form of these adjectives (Kobiljanskij 1953, as cited in Mel'čuk 1985, 173; Yadroff 1999, 147–149; Rakhlin 2003; Nevins and Bailyn 2008).

By contrast, the assumption that the noun *rjad* bears NGEN in both constructions in (114) is crucial to the broader claims of this monograph. The idea that nouns assign genitive because they *are* genitive is one of the central arguments for the claim that the case categories are in fact just the syntactic categories. If the noun in a paucal construction does not bear NGEN morphology after all, this argument vanishes.

Any discussion of the problem should begin with an acknowledgment that no proposal is likely to be able to *predict* the anomalous behavior of the five nouns that display the stress shift in (114). They share no independent common feature that distinguishes them from other nouns of the same declension class that do not behave anomalously. (In fact, the noun *šar* 'sphere' that normally exhibits anomalous suffixal stress in a paucal construction loses this property when used as a mathematical term, as noted by Zaliznjak (1977, 528).) The strongest argument that could ever favor one analysis over another must therefore concern *degree of anomaly*: to what extent does a given proposal provide an independently motivated pigeonhole into which the anomaly fits?

Proposals like that of Zaliznjak and his successors that posit distinct cases for *rjád-a* in (114a) and *rjad-á* in (114b) make no predictions about what form these case suffixes will take. These proposals therefore face the challenge of explaining why the form taken by nouns in nominative paucal constructions is segmentally identical to the genitive singular across all declension classes and genders. A proposal like the current one that identifies both forms as genitive has the advantage here, because it predicts segmental identity. On the other hand, it needs to offer an account of the stress shift.

In fact, the proposal developed in this monograph does contain a pigeonhole into which the exceptional stress pattern of nouns like *rjad* can be fit. Although the NGEN suffix in both the adnominal construction of (114a) and the paucal construction of (114b) takes the default form (-*a*, for declension class 1) expected of any case morpheme that is not [−SINGULAR], these two instances of -*a* do differ in number. The -*a* suffixed to N in the adnominal construction of (114a) is a [+SINGULAR] variant of NGEN, reflecting the fact that the noun itself entered the derivation with the property [+SINGULAR] and therefore receives [+SINGULAR] variants of the case suffixes that attach to it in the course of the derivation. The -*a* suffixed to N in the paucal construction of (114b), on the other hand, is a *numberless* variant of NGEN (as the gloss for (114a) indicated, with malice aforethought). This -*a* is a realization of "primeval" NGEN, which made a noun out of a root in the lexicon; and no other morphology has overwritten it in the course of the syntactic derivation.

As it happens, idiosyncratic number-dependent stress shifts are common in the Russian nominal system. In declension class 1, to which the five nouns like *rjad* belong, approximately 50 nouns with an otherwise normal declensional paradigm show a stress shift from stem to suffix in the plural: for example, *nós-u, nós-e, nós-om* 'nose-DAT/PREP/INSTR.SG' versus *nos-ám, nos-áx, nos-ámi* 'nose-DAT/PREP/INSTR.PL' (Garde 1980, 183–184).[5]

Strikingly, all five nouns of the *rjad* group belong to this group as well: *rjád-u, rjád-e, rjád-om* 'row-DAT/PREP/INSTR.SG' versus *rjad-ám, rjad-áx, rjad-ámi* 'row-DAT/PREP/INSTR.PL'. All that needs to be said about the five nouns that behave like *rjad* is that *the stress shift that they exhibit in the plural is exceptionally extended to numberless forms*—in contrast to other nouns of the stress-shifting class that group their numberless forms with the singular. We may conclude that the stress shift seen in (114b) is *not* a phenomenon peculiar to paucal constructions. Consequently, it does not motivate the postulation of a special case or number paradigm.[6]

8.5   Loose End: Prepositions That Appear to Assign N_{GEN}

Just as we needed to acknowledge the existence of prepositions that appear to assign V_{ACC} in section 7.3, so we must note the existence of prepositions that appear to assign N_{GEN}—and for the same reasons. The apparent existence of N_{GEN}-assigning prepositions threatens the claim that the syntactic categories and the cases should be identified.

For many of the expressions listed in Russian dictionaries as "prepositions that govern the genitive," there is an easy solution to this problem. These prepositions are transparently complex, consisting of an independently attested preposition (typically *v* 'in', *na* 'on', or *po* 'along') followed by a morpheme that independently occurs as a noun and bears its own case suffix. Examples include *v-vidu* 'in view of' (< 'in view-PREP.SG'), *v-mesto* 'instead of' (< 'into place-ACC.SG'), *vo-krug* 'around' (< 'into circle-ACC.SG'), *na-sčët* 'concerning' (< 'onto account-ACC.SG'), *po-verx* 'on top of' (< 'up.against top-ACC.SG'). In other cases, the second component is not an independently occurring noun in the modern language, but bears a case suffix that allows it to be parsed as a probable noun. For example, the second component of *v-nutri* 'inside (locative)' and *v-nutr'* 'inside (directional)' is clearly the same morpheme in each case: a class 3 noun *nutr'* 'interior' that bears P_{LOC} morphology in the first example and the kind of morphology expected of direct objects in the second. Despite the fact that the word *nutr'* is hardly used in the contemporary language except as a component of *vnutri* and *vnutr'* (it is listed as an alternative form of *nutro* 'interior' in Dal's historical dictionary and appears in three relevant citations found in the Russian National Corpus), this is clearly the correct analysis, since it makes immediate sense of the semantic distinction between the two expressions as an instance of the same alternation seen in (90): [_{PP} *v*_P [_{NP} *nutr-i* DP]] versus [_{DIRP} DIR_V [_{DP} *v*_P *nutr-'* DP]]. *Po-zadi* 'behind' presents a similar case, consisting of an independently occurring preposition and the P_{PREP} (prepositional case) form of a class 3 noun *zad'* that does not otherwise exist, but shares a root with a large number of words that are used independently—and there are other examples as well.

Can a similar analysis be extended to *all* other prepositions that govern the genitive? If one is willing to accept some startlingly creative (and philologically offensive) morpheme divisions for which synchronic support is otherwise lacking, a number of other examples can be analyzed in much the same fashion as those just discussed: for example, *pro-tiv* 'against, opposite from', *o-kolo* 'near', *po-sle* 'after'. In each instance, the material before the hyphen is a preposition of the language, even though the material after the hyphen is otherwise unknown.[7] In other cases, the existence of a P + N paraphrase for a seemingly monomorphemic preposition might be taken (as it is in much current work) as support for a phrasal analysis. An example is *krome* 'except', with an equally common P + N paraphrase *za isključeniem* 'with the exception of'; both take a genitive DP. Finally, directional prepositions that denote 'motion from' uniformly take a genitive DP: *iz* 'from', *ot* 'from', and *s* 'down from'. Here one might imagine that the same Dɪʀ posited in our discussion of accusative-governing prepositions might take a null noun whose meaning is exclusionary ('complement set of') as its object, with this noun in turn assigning Nɢᴇɴ to its complement: [Dɪʀᵥ [Cᴏᴍᴘʟᴇᴍᴇɴᴛ-sᴇᴛ-ᴏꜰɴ DP]].[8]

A residue remains, which includes several of the most common prepositions of the language: *bez* 'without', *dlja* 'for', *do* 'up to', *mimo* 'past', *u* 'at, by, belonging to'. Though a fuller analysis of the syntax associated with these prepositions might reveal a nominal component, it is also possible that the objects of these prepositions bear Nɢᴇɴ for some other reason. I leave the matter open.[9]

9 Feature Assignment and the Notion "Prototype"

9.1 Number in Adnominal Paucal Constructions

One important detail of the Russian adnominal genitive remains unaccounted for. I will first sketch a resolution that involves a modification of the view of FA taken so far. I will then suggest that this modification might in turn shed light on the parameter that distinguishes languages like Russian with rich case morphology from "non-case-marking" languages such as English or French.

When a paucal nominal phrase is merged as an adnominal, not only are all accessible elements of the paucal marked with NGEN morphology, but also this morphology is uniformly *plural*. In particular, plural NGEN morphology is present on the noun of the paucal construction. Recall that this noun entered the derivation numberless, so the fact that it bears a plural version of NGEN morphology within an adnominal DP is unexpected. These facts were exemplified in (99a), repeated here with the surprising plural morphology boldfaced.

(115) **Paucal adnominal genitive DP (= (99a))**

krasivy-j   stol-ъ   [DP èt-ix   posledn-**ix**
beautiful-M.NOM.SG table-NOM.SG   these-GEN.PL   last-GEN.**PL**

dvu-**x**   molod-**yx**   aktër-**ov**]
DUAL-**GEN**   young-GEN.**PL** actor-GEN.**PL**

'these last two young actors' beautiful table'

We did, of course, face an almost identical problem in section 4.2, when we examined the morphology of POBL assigned to the elements of a paucal nominal—but if we apply the solution that worked for POBL to adnominal NGEN, a significant problem arises. Recall that the noun in an oblique paucal construction, like the embedded noun in (115), bears a plural version of its case morphology, as shown in (116) (once again, despite the fact that it entered the derivation numberless).

(116) **Paucal oblique DP (modeled on (3b))**

(k) [_{DP} èt-im   posledn-im   dvu-m   molod-ym

(to)   these-DAT.PL   last-DAT.PL   DUAL-DAT.PL   young-DAT.PL

aktër-**am**]

actor-DAT.**PL**

'to these last two young actors'

The plural morphology on the noun in (116) was attributed to number agreement, triggered by unvalued NBR features on the element responsible for assigning POBL case morphology to it. This element was assumed to be P itself. As discussed, when the unvalued NBR features of this element probe the paucal DP, the first goals that they meet are valued [−SINGULAR]. Consequently, its previously unvalued NBR features are valued [−SINGULAR], and plural POBL morphology is deposited on the numberless noun by FA, in accordance with rule (34).

This explanation for (116) cannot be straightforwardly extended to adnominal constructions such as (115), however, unless we revise some aspects of the proposed theory of FA. We have assumed that when α merges with β, α is directly responsible for the assignment of morphology to β. Consequently, if we learn that certain features of the morphology assigner are unvalued, it must be α itself that bears unvalued versions of these features. That conclusion could be maintained for POBL, since no data contradict the supposition that prepositions enter the derivation with unvalued NBR features. A comparable conclusion cannot be maintained for NGEN, however. Nouns clearly *do* enter the derivation knowing whether they are [−SINGULAR] or [+SINGULAR] (or numberless). This assumption was in fact crucial to the account of other aspects of the paucal construction, as can be seen by reexamining the presentation in (24).

Furthermore, if we are ultimately successful in analyzing prepositions that appear to assign NGEN as syntactically complex objects that contain a nominal (which actually assigns the genitive morphology), then the same considerations hold for these prepositions. When a preposition in this group takes a paucal DP, the morphosyntax of the DP is exactly the same as that seen in adnominals like the bracketed DP in (115). For example:

(117) **Paucal complement of (apparent) genitive-assigning P**

okolo   [_{DP} èt-ix   posledn-ix   dvu-x   molod-yx

near   this-GEN.PL   last-GEN.PL   DUAL-GEN   young-GEN.PL

aktër-**ov**]

actor-GEN.**PL**

'near these last two young actors'

Consequently, we must make two related revisions in our understanding of FA. First, in light of examples like (115) (and (117), under the analysis we hope to develop), we can no longer assume that what is copied onto β when it merges with α is the matrix of grammatical features of α itself, including its *values* for such features as NBR. Instead, what is copied must be a reduced, "least common denominator" feature matrix, whose part-of-speech features are valued, but whose other features are unvalued. I will call this reduced version of α the *prototype* of α, and notate it with a dot (e.g., α•).

(118) **Prototype**

A feature matrix α• is the *prototype* of a lexical item α whose part of speech is x if and only if

a. for every feature F of some lexical item in x, F ∈ α•; and

b. for every feature F ∈ α•, F is valued if and only if F is a part-of-speech feature.

What FA does when α merges with β is to *copy* α• *onto* β. It is α•, not α, whose unvalued features probe β, and it is α• that is directly responsible for morphology on the terminal elements of β. That is why this morphology reflects the part of speech of α, but reflects the NBR specification of β, in examples like (115) (and, we may now assume, (116) as well).

In addition, if it is the features of α•, and not the features of α itself, that probe β, FA must also specify the *specific structural position* occupied by α•, from which its unvalued features probe β. This position must c-command β, but it must not c-command α—if it did, the unvalued features of α• would enter an Agree relation with their valued counterparts on α, quite the wrong result. We conclude, therefore, that FA merges α• directly with β, as stated in (119).

(119) **Feature Assignment (FA), version 5 of 6**

a. *Copying:* When α merges with β, forming [α α β], if α has satisfied its complementation requirements and is designated as a feature assigner for β, *its prototype α• is immediately merged with β, forming* [α α [β α• β]].

b. *Realization:* α• is realized as morphology on all accessible lexical items dominated by β.

We can now explain why the NGEN morphology assigned to the N of the paucal adnominal in (115) is plural (*aktër-ov*), even though the higher N 'table' ultimately responsible for NGEN assignment to the adnominal is singular. Though the N is singular, its prototype N• is unvalued for NBR. Its NBR features receive the value [−SINGULAR] by probing and agreeing with the adnominal DP. From its position as a sister to the adnominal, N• assigns morphology to the terminal elements of the DP it has been merged with, just as I have been claiming throughout this monograph. Because N• now bears [–SINGULAR], it will assign the plural version of NGEN morphology to the otherwise number-less N of a paucal construction, as required under rule (34). Note that the same account can now be given for the POBL example in (116) as well. Regardless of whether P itself is lexically valued for NBR (a question that is now irrelevant and perhaps untestable), its prototype P• is unvalued for NBR (by definition), and FA applies as above. In direct object position, where the requirements for assignment of VACC are met, V• will behave the same way.

9.2   Overt Prototypes in Languages without Case Morphology

At this point, one might reasonably object that the revision to FA developed in section 9.1 is undermotivated, having been developed solely to solve the problem of nominal number morphology on one lexical item of (115). Is there any *independent* evidence that merger of α with β is followed by merger of α• with β, as we have argued?

In fact, if the second clause of FA (119b) is rewritten so as to permit some degree of cross-linguistic variation in how features assigned by (119a) are realized, independent evidence may indeed be found. Copying without neces-sary "realization as morphology on all accessible lexical items" might offer an analysis of the freestanding "little words" that serve so often as the coun-terparts to case morphology in languages like French or English that largely lack this morphology. Suppose, for example, that N merges with DP as in (115), triggering the secondary merger of N• with DP, as required by the first clause of FA, (119a). Now suppose that in some configurations in some lan-guages, this copying is *not* followed by realization of the prototype as mor-phology on the lexical items of DP. Instead, N• is realized in situ, as a free or bound morpheme attached to the adnominal DP itself. The result might provide a partial theory of morphemes like French *de* and English *of*, and their relation to NGEN morphology in languages like Russian—namely, that they are instances of NGEN that have not undergone the second of the two processes given in (119), but are instead realized in situ.

(120) **Nonmorphological N• in French?**

la	table$_N$	[$_{DP}$ **de**$_N$•	[ces	deux	jeunes	acteurs]]
the	table	**of**	these	two	young	actors

One approach to this possibility might view Russian-style realization of a prototype as morphology on the lexical items of its sister as the limiting case of a more general rule that realizes a prototype on the *smallest available* subconstituents of its sister. We might then revise the second clause of FA as shown in (121b).

(121) **Feature Assignment (FA), version 6 of 6**

    a. *Copying:* When α merges with β, forming $[_\alpha\ \alpha\ \beta]$, if α has satisfied its complementation requirements and is designated as a feature assigner for β, its prototype $\alpha^\bullet$ is immediately merged with β, forming $[_\alpha\ \alpha\ [_\beta\ \alpha^\bullet\ \beta]]$.

    b. *Realization: A prototype $x^\bullet$ is realized adjacent to the smallest available element dominated by its sister.*

What I intend by the phrase *smallest available* is a downward-branching search of the prototype's sister for the smallest elements on which the resources of the language allow the prototype to be realized. Sometimes this search might fail completely, and no unacceptability necessarily results. We have already noted, for example, that certain parts of speech such as prepositions and verbs simply fail to allow the realization of case morphology in Russian. An adnominal PP in Russian, for example, shows no sign of genitive case morphology assigned to its head by N, and no unacceptability accrues as a consequence. Japanese is different in this respect, requiring genitive case morphology in exactly this circumstance.

(122) **Genitive morphology realized on adnominal PP (Japanese)**

    $[_{PP}$ Nihon-kara-**no**]   [kagaku-no]   gakusei

       Japan-from-GEN   chemistry-GEN   student

    'a student of chemistry from Japan'

Likewise, chapter 8 discussed the fact that Spell-Out of an adnominal DP renders it opaque to FA after merger with N (and assignment of NGEN). A search that encounters a spelled-out domain might attempt to realize a prototype adjacent to the entire domain (a possibility to which I return shortly), but will not be able to realize the prototype inside the domain.

On this view, languages like Russian or Lardil with overt case morphology are simply languages that allow the realization of prototypes as word-level morphology. Languages like French are languages that lack (or mostly lack) this option for realizing prototypes. (French clitic pronouns do show case distinctions.) If the words of a phrase in a particular language are incapable of realizing prototypes as word-level morphology, but the language does have the ability to realize the prototype at the maximal-projection level, it will do so—and the result will be elements like French *de*, which behaves as an adphrasal realization of the same NGEN that shows up as word-level morphology in Russian.

Recall now the proposal that has been crucial to the present analysis of Russian paucal and quantifier constructions: that Russian nouns are "born genitive." Since the genitive property that they are born with shows up as case morphology, I proposed that "primeval NGEN" is an element assigned in the lexicon that categorizes a root as a noun. I stated this proposal in (6), repeated here.

(123) **"Primeval genitive" conjecture (= (6))**
    NGEN categorizes a Russian root as a noun (in the lexicon).

If prototype categories exist, and if they behave in the manner described in this chapter, it is natural to view morphemes like the instance of "primeval NGEN" that categorizes a root as a noun as prototype categories. On this view, the Russian root √*aktër* 'actor', for example, merges in the lexicon with NGEN• to form the noun *aktër-GEN•*, and the unvalued φ-features of the prototype (e.g., feminine gender) receive their value from the root (by the rule Agree). Because Russian is a language with word-level case morphology, the prototype (if not overwritten by additional case suffixes) will be realized as morphology on the noun: *aktër-a* 'actor-NGEN'.

Let us now imagine that a language like French lacks the general ability to realize prototypes at the word level, but does have the ability to realize prototypes phrasally, at the level of the maximal projection. If this is the case, then when NGEN is added to a root like √*acteur* 'actor' to form a noun, it will not be realized as a word-level case affix—but may be realized as an instance of *de* prefixed to NP. Indeed, it is a striking fact about French that *de* is found prefixed to NP in many of the very same QUANT constructions where Russian shows "primeval genitive" morphology on N and adnominal dependents. If French is simply Russian minus the ability to realize an NGEN prototype as morphology on a lexical item, but with the ability to realize it on a maximal projection, the realization of NGEN on the head of an NP will be an NP-level occurrence of *de*.[1]

(124) **French QUANT construction (nominative environment)**
    a. beaucoup [NP **de**N• jeunes   acteurs]
        many   **of**   young.PL   actor.PL
        'many young actors'
    b. *Compare Russian*
        mnogo   [NP molod-yx   aktër-**ov**N•]
        many   young-GEN.PL actor-**GEN.PL**

Suppose now that the One-Suffix Rule is generalized to cover phrase-level as well as word-level occurrences of prototypes.

(125) **The One-Prototype Rule (replaces the One-Suffix Rule in (7))**[2]
       In the configuration $[_\beta n\ x\ [_\beta n\ y\ \dots\ \beta\ \dots]]$ (order irrelevant), where x
       and y are the realization of prototypes, delete y.

We now expect the addition of D to a nonquantificational NP to generally
suppress *de* in French, just as it suppresses NGEN morphology in Russian. The
realization of French D might be null in some circumstances, as it is in some
declension classes of Russian.

(126) **French QUANT construction (nominative environment)**
a. ces   D $[_{NP}$ D• ⊗$_{N}$• jeunes   acteurs]   (*ces jeunes acteurs*)
   these   – of   young.PL actor.PL
   'these young actors'
b. *Compare Russian*
   èti   D $[_{NP}$ molod-⊗$_{N}$•-ye$_{D}$•   aktër-(ov$_{N}$•) – y$_{D}$•]   (*èti molodye aktëry*)
   these   young-(GEN.PL)-NOM.PL actor-(GEN.PL)-NOM.PL
   'these young actors'

What saves *de* from suppression in (124a) might then be the same QUANT-
seeking property of D that saves NGEN morphology from suppression in its
Russian counterpart (124b), and possibly the same QUANT-to-D movement as
well. The null D• element that would be the French counterpart to DNOM
morphology in Russian is prefixed to *beaucoup* itself.

(127) **French QUANT construction (nominative environment)**

$[_{DP}$ D + [D$^{\bullet}$ beaucoup] $[_{NP}$ de$_{N}$• __ jeunes acteurs]]

Because French lacks a distinct class of paucals, a linguist specializing in
French would be very unlikely to arrive at the analysis sketched in (127) on
the basis of French evidence alone. On the other hand, there are so many other
similarities between the Russian and French nominal systems, particularly as
they concern quantificational elements like *beaucoup/mnogo*, that it may well
be profitable for the analysis of each language to be informed by the results
achieved by studying the other. Both languages, for example, have a "genitive-
of-negation" construction.[3] In both languages, the class of nonnumeral quantifiers that behave like *beaucoup/mnogo* is roughly the same—including the
word for *how many*, which may separate from its NP under *wh* in both languages, obeying many of the same constraints (Pesetsky 1982; Obenauer 1984;
Podobryaev 2010). Furthermore, although numeral constructions do not
straightforwardly behave like *beaucoup* in French, since they do not normally
contain an instance of *de* between the numeral and NP, they do take a genitive

clitic when the NP is pronominal—and a *de* surfaces obligatorily before a right-dislocated NP corresponding to such a pronoun (Milner 1978).

Outside the domain of NP, there are other candidates for the status of prototype that might merit investigation. For example, the distribution of differential object-marking prepositions such as "accusative *a*" in Spanish recalls the realization of VACC morphology in Russian and might be viewed as a phrase-level realization of V•. Comparable proposals for POBL might provide an analysis of the final component of complex prepositional expressions such as the second component of English *next to, instead of,* and the like.

The kinds of elements sometimes classified as "linkers" may have a similar character (Collins 2003; Den Dikken and Singhapreecha 2004; Baker and Collins 2006; Den Dikken 2006). For example, the nominal-internal raising studied by Den Dikken and his colleagues that triggers the occurrence of English *of* and its counterparts in constructions like *that idiot of a doctor* or French *une pizza de chaude* 'a hot pizza' (lit. 'a pizza of hot') might indeed serve simply as a host for the moved element, as suggested in the works cited. Alternatively, one might imagine a connection more analogous to that proposed here for the presence of NGEN morphology when Russian QUANT raises to D. For example, *une pizza de chaude* might involve raising of N to D, with the requirements of D in this construction blocking the overwriting of N• (*de*) by D•.

Consequently, though firm conclusions must await more detailed investigation, it is possible that the distribution of elements like French *de* and English *of* will support the notion "prototype" cross-linguistically—and in particular, the following proposals:

1. that it is α• (not α itself) that FA assigns as a sister to β after α merges with β;

2. that a root R is assigned to syntactic category α by the merger of α• with R; and

3. that prototypes are not necessarily realized as word-level morphology, but are realized at the lowest structural level that the language and construction permit—which is sometimes phrase-level.

9.3   An Unresolved Puzzle of Lardil Case Stacking

The possibility that the element assigned by FA may be realized at the maximal projection level as well as at the word level suggests another way in which a case-marking language that shows the effects of the One-Suffix Rule may nonetheless display overt case stacking in certain environments. In this section,

I argue that one of the peculiarities of Lardil case stacking discussed in section 3.2 instantiates this very possibility. In the next section, I conclude by noting a Russian construction that might represent an instance of the same thing—so (if this speculation is correct) Russian has overt case stacking after all.

Lardil was discussed in section 3.2 as an example of a language with overt case stacking that also shows effects of the One-Suffix Rule. As analyzed in that section (building on proposals in Richards 2007, 2013), Lardil morphology provides evidence not only for the assignment of NGEN, DNOM, POBL, and VACC much as in Russian, but also for the assignment of TFUT morphology by T.

Let us briefly review the facts and analysis presented in the earlier discussion of Lardil. Recall that NGEN, POBL, and TFUT morphology may visibly cooccur with morphology assigned later in the derivation (yielding overt case stacking), as seen in (128)–(130).

(128) ACC, INSTR **stacking outside GEN (Lardil)**

   a. *GEN-ACC stacking (= (14a))*

     Ngada   derlde   marun-ngan-i   wangalk-i.

     I   break   boy-GEN-ACC   boomerang-ACC

     'I broke the boy's boomerang.'

     (Richards 2007; 2013, 49 ex. (20a))

   b. *GEN-INSTR stacking (= (14b))*

     Ngada latha   karnjin-i   [marun-ngan-ku   maarn-ku].

     I   spear wallaby-ACC   boy-GEN-INSTR   spear-INSTR

     'I speared the wallaby with the boy's spear.'

     (Richards 2007; 2013, 43 ex. (3))

   c. *GEN-FUT stacking (= (17))*

     Ngada   derlde-thu   marun-ngan-ku   wangalk-u.

     I   break-FUT   boy-GEN-FUT   boomerang-FUT

     'I will break the boy's boomerang.'

     (Richards 2007; 2013, 49 ex. (20b))

(129) INSTR-FUT **stacking (Lardil) (= (16b))**

     Ngada   nguthunguthu-r   warnawu-thur   dulnhuka-r

     I   slowly-FUT   cook-FUT   month.fish-FUT

     beerr-uru-r   nyith-uru-r.

     ti-tree-INSTR-FUT   fire-INSTR-FUT

     'I will slowly cook the month fish on a fire of ti-tree wood.'

     (Richards 2007; 2013, 48 ex. (16b))

(130) **FUT-ACC stacking (Lardil) (= (18))**

Kara	nyingki	kurri	kiin-i	mutha-n	thungal-i,
Q	you	see	that-ACC	big-ACC	tree-ACC

[ngithun-i   kirdi-thuru-Ø]?
I.GEN-ACC   cut-FUT-ACC

'Do you see that big tree, which I am going to cut down?'
(Richards 2007; 2013, 52 ex. (29a))

On the other hand, VACC is always deleted when it is not the outermost morpheme, as the presence of VACC morphology in a relative clause modifying a FUT-marked NP showed us. The key observation supporting this claim (due to Richards and Hale) was the fact that VACC morphology *should* appear inside FUT throughout both the NP and its relative clause, but does not.

(131) **FUT appears on direct-object nominal, ACC on elements of relative clause (Lardil) (= (19))**

Ngada	kurri-thu	karnjin-ku	[ngithun	thabuji-kan-i
I	see-FUT	wallaby-FUT	my	older.brother-GEN-ACC

la-tharrba-Ø]
spear-NONFUT-ACC

'I want to see the wallaby that my older brother speared.'
(Richards 2007; 2013, 52 ex. (30))

I attributed the failure of TFUT morphology to appear on the elements of the relative clause to an inability of tense morphology assignment to penetrate an independently tensed domain. Following Richards, I took the presence of VACC morphology on these elements as evidence that the higher verb has assigned VACC to its object—just as it does in nonfuture examples where FUT is never assigned, and VACC morphology appears throughout the entire object DP.

(132) **VACC assigned to a direct object extends into relative clause as well (Lardil) (= (18))**

Kara	nyingki	kurri	kiin-i	mutha-n	thungal-i,	[ngithun-i
Q	you	see	that-ACC	big-ACC	tree-ACC	I.GEN-ACC

kirdi-thuru-Ø]?
cut-FUT-ACC

'Do you see that big tree, which I am going to cut down?'
(Richards 2007; 2013, 52 ex. (29a))

The absence of VACC morphology inside TFUT on the direct object in (131) (i.e., the fact that the object is 'wallaby-FUT' and not 'wallaby-ACC-FUT') could now be attributed to the One-Suffix Rule, operating in Lardil just as it does in Russian. Note that examples like (132), where ACC is stacked outside a tense morpheme, show that Vᴀᴄᴄ deletes only when internal to a second suffix, just as the One-Suffix Rule states.

I proposed that case stacking arises when certain case suffixes are marked as undeletable, thus not falling under the One-Suffix Rule. I will continue to assume that this is the reason why we see stacking outside ɪɴsᴛʀ and ꜰᴜᴛ. Stacking outside ɢᴇɴ presents a somewhat different picture, however. Here, I will argue, an empirical puzzle in Lardil converges with a theory-internal puzzle posed by the present analysis of the sources of case morphology.

The theory-internal puzzle concerns the distribution of visible Nɢᴇɴ morphology. If we attribute case stacking outside of genitive morphology to the nondeletability of Nɢᴇɴ (i.e., if Nɢᴇɴ, like Pᴏʙʟ and Tꜰᴜᴛ, falls outside the One-Suffix Rule), and we simultaneously hold to the doctrine that "you are what you assign," we expect not only the possessor nominal, but also the possessee NP with which it merges, to show Nɢᴇɴ morphology. If we attribute the absence of Nɢᴇɴ on the possessee to overwriting by Dɴᴏᴍ or some higher case-assigner, we contradict the claim that Nɢᴇɴ is nondeletable and lose the proposed account of stacking outside Nɢᴇɴ.

The empirical puzzle arises when we examine the morphology found inside Nɢᴇɴ-marked phrases. Though the subconstituents of a possessor nominal all bear the Nɢᴇɴ morphology assigned by the possessee N with which it merged, stacking of other case morphology only appears on the head noun. To begin with, Hale (1998, 199) and Richards (2007, 2013) note that though a possessor in a Vᴀᴄᴄ-marked or Tꜰᴜᴛ-marked DP will bear stacked Vᴀᴄᴄ or Tꜰᴜᴛ outside the expected Nɢᴇɴ, a possessor of this possessor will not bear this stacked morphology, as (134) shows. I will need to attribute this observation to a haplology avoidance rule that deletes an Nɢᴇɴ suffix when it immediately follows another instance of Nɢᴇɴ.

(133) **Genitive Haplology Rule**
       Nɢᴇɴ → Ø / __ Nɢᴇɴ

The problem runs deeper, however. Not only does a possessor within a possessor fail to bear two instances of Nɢᴇɴ, it may not bear any stacked morphology whatsoever, as (134a–b) show. Furthermore, as (135) shows, the same is true of a demonstrative within a possessor, which bears Nɢᴇɴ but not the additional stacked morphology that the head noun bears. Klokeid (1976, 524) states the generalization as follows: "[O]nce a [case] category is assigned to a possessor, it does not distribute to the dependents of that possessor,"

(134) **Possessor within a possessor does not show stacking (Lardil)**

 a. Ngada derlde [[marun-ngan thabuji-kan-i]
   I   break boy-GEN-(*ACC) older.brother-GEN-ACC
   wangalk-i].
   boomerang-ACC
   'I broke the boy's older brother's boomerang.'
   (Richards 2007; 2013, 50 ex. (24))

 b. Ngada derlde-thu [[marun-ngan thabuji-kan-ku]
   I   break-FUT boy-GEN-(*FUT) older.brother-GEN-FUT
   wangalk-u].
   boomerang-FUT
   'I will break the boy's older brother's boomerang.'
   (Richards 2007; 2013, 51 ex. (25))

(135) **Demonstrative within a possessor DP does not show stacking**

 Ngada kurri-kun [[kiin-nga   bidngen-ngan-in] karnan-in
 I.NOM see-ACTUAL that-GEN-(*ACC) woman-GEN-ACC tall-ACC
 kambin-in].
 son-ACC
 'I saw that woman's tall son.'
 (Klokeid 1976, 524 ex. (142))

In example (131), the absence of stacked V$_{ACC}$ morphology on *ngithun* 'my', the possessor of the genitive subject of the relative clause, suggests that the puzzle is not limited to possessors, but probably applies to all N$_{GEN}$-marked nominals.

Somewhat tentatively (due to limitations of the available data), I suggest that the theory-internal puzzle concerning N$_{GEN}$ deletion and the empirical puzzle raised by (131) and (134)–(135) have the same solution—and that the solution is closely related to the discussion in this chapter and its predecessor.

Let us start with some observations about Lardil phases, taking this chapter's proposals as background. The fact that V$_{ACC}$ morphology assigned to a DP object also penetrates its relative clause suggests that such clauses are not phasal in Lardil, or at least do not interact with FA as phases do in Russian.[4] If relative clauses were phasal, we would not be surprised by the assignment of N$_{GEN}$ morphology inside the clause upon merger with the host noun, but we do not expect V$_{ACC}$ to be able to penetrate the relative clause, since it would have undergone Spell-Out immediately after merging with N. Similarly, the fact that T$_{FUT}$ morphology assigned to vP may penetrate an object DP suggests that DPs are not generally phasal either, or at least do not interact with FA as expected if they were. If DPs were generally phasal, we would not be surprised by the assignment of VACC morphology when DP merges with V, or POBL morphology when DP merges with P, but this merger should also trigger Spell-Out, preventing subsequent assignment of morphology by TFUT.

On the other hand, genitive DPs behave differently. If we ignore the head noun, and direct our attention to other elements such as the most embedded possessors in (134a–b), the possessor of the relative clause subject in (131), and the demonstrative within the possessor in (135), genitive DPs appear to behave exactly as the theory of this chapter leads us to expect from a phasal category. The morphology assigned by the N with which the phase has merged is visible, but no subsequent morphology has penetrated the domain. This suggests the following conclusion:

(136) **Phasal interactions with FA in Lardil**
       Genitive-marked DP interacts as a phase with FA. Other DPs and relative clauses do not.

How then do we explain the stacked cases that appear on the head noun of genitive DPs in the same examples? I propose that these are instances of case morphology assigned not to the lexical items contained by the genitive DP, but to the DP as a whole. In other words, the case affixes stacked outside NGEN morphology, despite their affixal status, are *phrase-level* realizations of proto-types like French *de*.

We are now free to assume that NGEN morphology (unlike PINSTR and TFUT) is subject to the One-Suffix Rule after all, and does delete when the form to which NGEN has been suffixed receives a second case suffix. That is why a possessee noun may assign NGEN to a possessor DP, yet bear no genitive morphology itself. Once the possessor DP receives NGEN from the possessee, the possessor undergoes Spell-Out, and its genitive morphology is forever frozen and undeletable. When D merges with the full NP formed from the possessor and possessee, DNOM overwrites NGEN morphology on the possessee, but can no longer affect NGEN morphology on the possessor DP.

How, then, can the possessor DP receive additional case morphology, as it does in (128)–(130), and why does NGEN on the possessor not delete when this happens? The answer is that a prototype assigned by a higher element is being realized at the phrase level, rather than the word level (i.e., on the possessor DP as a whole)—and that phrase-level morphology in Lardil is homophonous with the word-level morphology that the prototype *would* have assigned to the possessor's lexical items, had the possessor not been frozen when spelled out. That is why this morphology is realized only once, at the periphery of the possessor DP, and is not spread to that DP's subconstituents.[5]

Consider, for example, how the derivation produces the object DP 'that woman's tall son' in (135). (For ease of exposition, I will use English glosses in lieu of Lardil morphemes.) First, the DP *that woman* merges as a possessor with the N′ *tall son*. The N′ possessee assigns NGEN to *that woman*, which places genitive morphology on both *that* and *woman*. The possessor DP *that woman* immediately undergoes Spell-Out (since genitive DPs are phasal), which ensures that the NGEN morphology of the possessor will never be over-written. Any new morphology attached to this DP will have to be realized at the phrase level. I indicate spelled-out domains with shading, show the pos-sessee with the NGEN morphology it was born with, and show the adjective *tall* with the NGEN morphology it will have received by FA from *son*.

Step 1: [$_{NP}$ [$_{DP}$ that-GEN woman-GEN] [$_{N'}$ tall-GEN son-GEN]]

Next, D merges with the newly formed NP. It assigns DNOM (phonologically null in Lardil) to its sister NP, which is assigned as a phrase-level affix to the possessor *that woman* and as a word-level affix to *tall* and to *son*. By the One-Suffix Rule, DNOM overwrites GEN on *tall* and on *son*, but leaves genitive morphology on *that woman* untouched, since the possessor DP was already spelled out.

Step 2: [$_{DP}$ D [$_{NP}$ [$_{DP}$ that-GEN woman-GEN]-NOM•

[$_{N'}$ tall-G̶E̶N̶-NOM son-G̶E̶N̶-NOM]]]

When this newly formed DP merges with V, the verb assigns VACC to its complement. The accusative morphology assigned by V will be assigned at the phrase level to the already spelled-out possessor *that woman*—so it will be realized only once, on the noun at the right edge of this phrase. On the other hand, it will be assigned as word-level morphology to *tall* and to *son*, just as DNOM assigned its morphology. I assume that the inner affix NOM deletes throughout the DP by the One-Suffix Rule (vacuously, since it is pho-nologically null).

Step 3: V [$_{DP}$ D [$_{NP}$ [$_{DP}$ that-GEN woman-GEN]-NO̶M̶•-ACC•

[$_{N'}$ tall-̶G̶E̶N̶-N̶O̶M̶-ACC son-G̶E̶N̶-NO̶M̶-ACC]]]

A similar reasoning explains the impossibility of case stacking on the pos-sessor of a genitive DP, such as the possessive DP in *boy's older.brother's boomerang* in (134a). First, the DP *boy* merges as a possessor with the N (or N′) *older.brother*. *Older.brother* assigns NGEN to the DP *boy*, which immedi-ately undergoes Spell-Out (since genitive DPs are phasal). This freezes the genitive morphology on *boy*, so it will never be overwritten. Any new morphol-ogy attached to the DP *boy* will have to be phrase-level.

Step 1: [$_{NP}$ [$_{DP}$ boy-GEN] [$_N$ older.brother-GEN]]

Next, D merges with the newly formed NP. It assigns DNOM (phonologically null) to its sister NP, which is assigned as a phrase-level affix to the possessor *boy-GEN* and as a word-level affix to *older.brother-GEN*. By the One-Suffix Rule, DNOM overwrites GEN on *older.brother* but cannot do the same to GEN on *boy*, since *boy-GEN* has already undergone Spell-Out.

Step 2: [$_{DP}$ D [$_{NP}$ [$_{DP}$ boy-GEN]-NOM• [$_N$ older.brother-GEN-NOM]]]]

This newly formed DP now merges as a possessor of the noun *boomerang*, which assigns NGEN to *boy's older.brother*. The One-Suffix Rule deletes NOM, and the Genitive Haplology Rule deletes the second of the two genitive affixes on *boy*.[6] The possessive DP spells out, and its remaining morphology is now frozen.

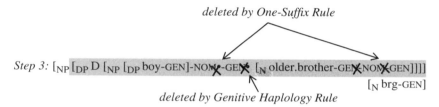

deleted by One-Suffix Rule

Step 3: [$_{NP}$ [$_{DP}$ D [$_{NP}$ [$_{DP}$ boy-GEN]-NOM•-GEN• [$_N$ older.brother-GEN-NOM-GEN]]]]
[$_N$ brg-GEN]

deleted by Genitive Haplology Rule

Merger of D to the structure just formed is followed by the assignment of DNOM (phrasally to the possessive DP) and the deletion of the NGEN morphology with which the noun *boomerang* was born, by the One-Suffix Rule.

Step 4:

[$_{DP}$ D [$_{NP}$ [$_{DP}$ D [$_{NP}$ [$_{DP}$ boy-GEN]-NOM•-GEN•
[$_N$ older.brother-GEN-NOM-GEN]]]]-NOM•[$_N$ brg-GEN-NOM]]

Crucially, when the DP formed in step 4 is merged as a complement of V, phrasal VACC will be affixed to *boy's older.brother* and word-level VACC will be affixed to *boomerang*, but the possessor of the possessor—*boy's*—will be left untouched by the One-Suffix Rule, since it is now deeply embedded in an already spelled-out and frozen domain—the correct result, as (134a) shows.

Step 5:

[$_{VP}$ V [$_{DP}$ D [$_{NP}$ [$_{DP}$ D [$_{NP}$ [$_{DP}$ boy-GEN]-NOM•-GEN•
[$_N$ older.brother-GEN-NOM-GEN]]]]-NOM•-ACC•[$_N$ brg-GEN-NOM-ACC]]]

If an instance of future tense merges later in the same derivation, TFUT will assign its morphology into the VP formed in step 5. Since nongenitive DPs are not phasal in Lardil, nothing will have been frozen since step 4, and TFUT morphology will overwrite ACC throughout step 5, yielding (134b), rather than (134a).

9.4   Overt Case Stacking in Russian?

The idea that FA adds an element to the sister of the feature assigner, before this element (the "prototype") is realized somewhere internal to the sister, was advanced at the beginning of this chapter to solve a problem with number agreement in Russian adnominal genitives. I proposed that N does not directly assign genitive morphology to its dependents, but assigns it indirectly—by first spawning a featurally reduced "prototype" that attaches to the dependent phrase, and that it is this prototype whose features end up as morphology on the smallest available elements of the phrase. I suggested that languages like French that show nonaffixal "little words" like *de* where languages like Russian have case morphology might be languages in which the prototype is realized overtly. I have now suggested that when Lardil case stacking involves affixation to a genitive-marked nominal, the outer cases have attached to an already spelled-out phrase, rather than to a lexical word. Case stacking is observed in these configurations precisely because morphology that has already been spelled out is frozen forever and cannot be affected by processes like the One-Suffix Rule.

As I noted when discussing the final revision of FA in (121), if a prototype finds a smallest accessible category within its sister, but the morphology or lexicon of the language provides no means to realize the prototype in this position, this failure of realization appears to cause no unacceptability. In this context, consider again a construction like (137a), in which D assigns DNOM to its sister NP, which is realized as word-level morphology on both 'beautiful' and 'table'. As discussed in chapter 8, Spell-Out of the adnominal possessor DP takes place immediately after the N 'table' assigns NGEN to it, so we understand why DNOM cannot be realized as word-level morphology on 'young' or 'actor'. We must now also exclude the possibility of realizing DNOM on the possessor DP as stacked morphology (or a free morpheme) at the phrase level—to which our answer has been a simple lack of lexical resources to do this in Russian. Likewise in (137b), where we see PDAT morphology assigned by 'to' to its object and realized at the word level on 'beautiful' and 'table', we attribute the inability of PDAT to also realize itself at the phrase level on the spelled-out possessor to a dearth of lexical resources. We appear to be forced to the conclusion that Russian is simply poorer than Lardil in these lexical resources and thus lacks the kind of case stacking that we have attributed to phrase-level realization of case morphology.

(137) **No phrase-level realization of case on the adnominal possessor in Russian?**

a. [_{DP} D [_{NP} krasivy-j   stol-ъ   [_{DP} molod-ogo   aktër-a]]]
                beautiful-M.NOM.SG table-NOM.SG   young-M.GEN.SG   actor-GEN.SG
     'the young actor's beautiful table'

b. [_{PP} k [_{DP} D [_{NP} krasiv-omu   stol-u   [_{DP} molod-ogo   aktër-a]]]]
          to   beautiful-M.DAT.SG table-DAT.SG   young-M.GEN.SG   actor-GEN.SG
     'to the young actor's beautiful table'

Nonetheless, viewed from the appropriate perspective, certain constructions in Russian may actually reveal a capacity to realize phrase-level case morphology on an adnominal DP after all, with the consequence that Russian might be more like Lardil than first appearances suggest. These constructions involve adnominal constituents that are often described as "adjectival," because they involve special morphology attached to their root (that could be considered adjective-forming) and show the same case, number, and gender as the noun with which they have merged—much like an adjective. An alternative view of these constructions, however, might see the special morphology attached to the root as a genitive suffix, and the additional "adjectival" morphology as stacked case.

One example involves special possessive words that can be formed from certain Russian proper names and nouns that identify people by family relationship such as *mama*, *papa*, *tëtja* 'aunt', and some others. These words are formed by the addition of the suffix *-in* (occasionally *-ov*) to a nominal base, which is followed by case morphology (with an unusual declension pattern that draws some of its suffixes from the nominal and others from the adjectival paradigm).

(138) **Examples of special possessive forms**

    a. tët-in-a   knig-a
         aunt-SUFFIX-F.NOM.SG   book-NOM.SG
         'Auntie's book'

    b. k   Maš-in-omu   dom-u
         to   Masha-SUFFIX-M.DAT.SG   house-DAT.SG
         'to Masha's house'

If we view the morpheme labeled "SUFFIX" in (138) as an instance of N_{GEN} morphology, rather than as an adjectivizer, then this construction is a Russian counterpart to the Lardil case-stacking constructions of (128), in which a (word-level) genitive suffix on a possessor noun is followed by a second (phrase-level) case suffix that marks the same case relations as the possessee. The special form that N_{GEN} morphology takes (*-in* instead of the genitive suffix -*y* otherwise used with *mama* and *Maša*) can then be understood as an allomorph used in case-stacking contexts. The One-Suffix Rule fails to apply to this suffix because the possessor has undergone Spell-Out after receiving genitive morphology from the possessee—again, just as in Lardil.

There is in fact evidence that forms such as these are treated as genitives, and not as adjectives. The possessors in (138a–b) consist of a single noun, which, under our Lardil-inspired analysis, bears both its own word-level NGEN morphology and the phrase-level DNOM and PDAT morphology assigned after the possessor has undergone Spell-Out. If a possessive form like those in (138a–b) forms part of a larger phrase, and these constructions truly are the Russian counterparts to Lardil case-stacking possessive constructions, then we should find NGEN morphology on the other members of the phrase—in its normal form, not the special case-stacking allomorph—and only the head or rightmost member of the possessive phrase should bear the morphology seen in (138a–b). Though the relevant constructions are colloquial and restricted in productivity, this is exactly what we find, as noted by Rappaport (to appear).

(139) **Multiword possessive phrases: Case stacking only on rightmost/ head noun (Russian)**

    a. **Tët-i**   **Maš-in-y**   **det-i**
        aunt-GEN.SG **Masha-SUFFIX-NOM.PL** **child-NOM.PL**
        žili   družno.
        lived   harmoniously
        'Aunt Masha's children lived harmoniously.'
        (from G. Oster, *Legendy i Mify Lavrovova Pereulka*, widely reprinted on the Web)

    b. Inogda djadja Jura i babuška […] tolkovali […]
        'Sometimes Uncle Yura and Grandma would chat …
        … pro   **djad-i**   **Jur-in-u**
        … about **uncle-GEN** **Yura-SUFFIX-FEM.ACC.SG**
        doček-u […]
        daughter-ACC.SG …
        … about Uncle Yura's daughter …'
        (from Alexai Varlamov, *Kupavna*, Novy Mir, pub. 2000; via Russian National Corpus)

Russian appears to restrict dependents of the special possessive to a single relationship noun ('aunt', 'uncle', etc.), as seen in (139a–b) (for unclear reasons)—but other Slavic languages are freer in this respect. In a study of these possibilities across Slavic, Corbett (1987) calls particular attention to the

West Slavic language Upper Sorbian, which allows a wider variety of dependents on the first member of the construction, including further possessives. As predicted, these dependents show genitive morphology, indicating clearly the genitive character of the special possessive form.

(140) **Multiword possessive phrases: Case stacking only on rightmost/ head noun (Upper Sorbian)**

    a. moj-eho   brat-ow-e   dźěć-i
        my-M.GEN.SG   brother-SUFFIX-NOM.PL   child-NOM.PL
        'my brother's children'
        (Corbett 1987, 300 ex. (1))

    b. w   naš-eho   nan-ow-ej   chěž-i
        in   our-M.GEN.SG   father-SUFFIX-FEM.LOC.SG   house-LOC.SG
        'in our father's house'
        (Corbett 1986, 1008 ex. (41))[7]

    c. Son-in-eho   nan-ow-y   přećel
        Sonja-SUFFIX-M.GEN.SG   father-SUFFIX-M.NOM.SG   friend.NOM.SG
        'Sonja's father's friend'
        (colloquial, not uniformly accepted; Toops 2008, 403)

    d. star-eje   žon-in-a   drast-a
        old-F.GEN.SG   woman-SUFFIX-F.NOM.SG   dress-NOM.SG
        'old woman's dress'
        (Corbett 1986, 1007 ex. (38))

I conclude that it is at least plausible to regard the Slavic possessive suffix conservatively glossed as "SUFFIX" above as an allomorph of GEN, which makes these possessive constructions close counterparts to Lardil case-stacking possessives.

Rappaport (to appear) presents a number of observations that suggest a similar analysis for first and second person possessive pronouns that do not contain a distinguishable possessive suffix, but share case, gender, and number morphology with their possessee (i.e., the Russian counterparts to *moj-* 'my' and *naš-* 'our' seen in (140a–b)). He notes, for example, that "simile expressions based on the preposition *kak* 'like, as' introduce a [nominal] agreeing in case with the standard of comparison .... When such a construction is applied to a possessive pronoun, the complement ... is a [nominal] in the genitive case."

(141) **Case agreement in simile expressions extends to possessive**
       pronouns

a. *NOM agreement in* **kak** *simile*

   On   letit   kak   ptic-**a**.
   he.**NOM**   flies   like   bird-**NOM**
   'He flies like a bird.'

b. *ACC agreement in* **kak** *simile*

   On   menj-**a**   ub'ët   kak   mux-**u**.
   he.**NOM** me-**ACC**   will.kill   like   fly-**ACC**
   'He will kill me like a fly.'

c. *DAT agreement in* **kak** *simile*

   Pomogaju   j-**emu**   kak   brat-**u**.
   I.help   him-**DAT**   like   brother-**DAT**
   'I am helping him as [I would help] a brother.'

d. *GEN agreement with possessive pronoun in* **kak** *simile*

   Vaš-a   perv-aja   zadač-a,   kak
   your.PL-F.NOM.SG   first-F.NOM.SG   task-NOM.SG   as
   Evropjec-**ev**,   budet …
   European-**GEN**.PL   will.be …
   'Your first task as Europeans will be …'
   (data from Rappaport, to appear)

Following Rappaport's proposal, we may give the same analysis for possessive pronouns as we have given for special possessors formed from nouns: they are (suppletive) genitive-marked forms that receive additional phrase-level morphology after Spell-Out.

Another possible instance of case stacking in Russian, for which much the same proposal can be advanced, is seen in compound modifiers that are derived from a higher numeral or paucal that has merged with a noun. Strikingly, the numeral appears in its genitive form.

(142) **Numeral + noun modifiers**

a. *dvuxètažnyj dom*   dv-**ux**   ètaž-n-yj
   'two-story house'   DUAL-**GEN**   floor-SUFFIX-M.NOM.SG

b. *Trëxgrošovaja opera* tr-**ëx**   groš-ov-aja
   'Threepenny Opera'   TRIAL-**GEN**   penny-SUFFIX-F.NOM.SG

c. *šestinedel'nyj kurs* šest-**i**   nedel'-n-yj
   'six-week course'   six-**GEN**   week-SUFFIX-M.NOM.SG

A traditional description would identify the morpheme glossed in (142) as "SUFFIX" as an adjectivizer—and indeed, the case suffixes that follow this morpheme are those normally found with adjectives (in contrast to the possessive suffix discussed above, whose declensional pattern is somewhat different). Suppose that instead we view this morpheme as a different kind of allomorph of NGEN, assigned by the head noun to an adnominal DP consisting of a numeral and a noun, for example, 'two-story'. The morphology on the numeral component of these compound modifiers is now expected. The first component of 'two-story' is *dv-ux* 'DUAL-GEN' in (142a) for the same reason it is *dv-ux* in (115): the rule FA has copied an NGEN prototype from the head noun 'house' onto the adnominal 'two stories', with exactly the same results. The NGEN prototype is valued plural by the plural phrase 'two houses' and is able to realize word-level genitive plural morphology on both 'two' and 'house'. At this point, the adnominal phrase undergoes Spell-Out, but as the derivation proceeds, the phrase as a whole acquires other case morphology, which is realized at the phrase level—and therefore appears only once, on 'house', like stacked case in Lardil possessors.[8]

9.5   Summary

This chapter began by taking up the puzzle posed by the plural morphology on genitive adnominal DPs that contain a paucal—in particular, plural morphology on the paucal and numberless noun in such phrases. The comparable puzzle for complements to P had been solved by the proposal that prepositions come unvalued for φ-features, and value these features by agreement with their DP complement. In the case of adnominal complements, the noun that assigns NGEN comes with its own φ-features, so plural morphology in the adnominal cannot result from the noun itself undergoing φ-feature agreement. To solve this problem, I proposed that feature assignment by a head proceeds in two stages: first copying onto its sister a "prototype" that is valued for part-of-speech features but unvalued for φ-features, then realizing this prototype on the smallest constituents that the language permits.

This revision does complicate the picture painted in previous chapters (where no "prototype" was posited), so several independent arguments were given for the reality of these prototype categories. In particular, the possibility of realizing the prototype in situ provided a theory of "small words" such as French *de*, whose syntax is so similar to case morphology in languages like Russian. The possibility of realizing the prototype at the phrase level offered an account of one type of case stacking in Lardil (stacking outside NGEN morphology), whose properties could not be attributed to simple undeletability of a case morpheme.

The discussion of Lardil, in turn, took us back to Russian, where the properties of several adnominal constructions now turned out to strongly recall the

Lardil constructions we had just discussed. This final section was more specu-
lative than most of this monograph. It remains to be seen whether a coherent
proposal about Russian allomorphy and declension class can be developed that
supports the suggestion that suffixes normally viewed as "adjectivizers" should
actually be categorized as allomorphs of NGEN. Having begun this monograph
with the somewhat counterintuitive suggestion (first advanced by Richards)
that Russian is a case-stacking language under the surface—a kind of "hidden
Lardil"—it seemed appropriate to end with the possibility that some of its
similarities to Lardil are not even so very hidden. If the proposal made here
proves to be sustainable, then even some surface forms of Russian show case
stacking, when viewed from the right perspective. Nonetheless, many details
of the proposal remain to be worked out in future research, so caution is
warranted.

10 Conclusions

Throughout this monograph, I have tried to operate at three levels simultaneously. At the highest level, the monograph has formulated and attempted to support a view of case morphology that eliminates the notion from linguistic theory, reducing the distinctions among cases to the independent distinctions among parts of speech. At the intermediate level, the monograph has presented a very particular view of Russian case morphology uniquely compatible with the monograph's lofty goals, and it has attempted to show that a series of seeming idiosyncrasies in the distribution of Russian case morphology can be explained under this view. At the lowest level, I have done my best to not shrink from the task of dealing with the bewildering array of factual details that Russian presents in this domain.

As always in linguistics, however, one's best is not good enough. A mere glance at the astonishing array of observations in works such as Mel'čuk 1985 (or a half-hour's questioning of a live Russian speaker) will at once make it clear how many puzzles and quirks remain undiscussed in this monograph. And as always, it is entirely possible that a different selection of these puzzles, or an attack on them from a fresh perspective, would yield conclusions different from those defended here. Nonetheless, I have conducted the research reported here with one idea in mind: that the picture of Russian that I develop can only be supported by careful attention to as much of the empirical picture as possible; and that the picture of (one corner of) Universal Grammar that I have attempted to support here can only be supported by the understanding we develop about the individual languages of the world, such as Russian.

In this light, it might be considered a defect of the proposals advanced in the preceding chapters that they partly rely on auxiliary proposals that are independent of the central ideas of this monograph concerning case and the syntactic categories: in particular, the movement operations that have been posited (on the part of NBR and QUANT) and the ordering of Merge, FA, and Spell-Out stipulated in (111). I am sympathetic to such objections. At the same time, I believe there is a logic to the findings reported in this monograph that mitigate this objection somewhat—albeit in a somewhat curious manner.

Let us imagine, for the sake of the argument, that the overall, intermediate-level proposal is true: that nouns are born genitive, that they and other elements assign their features in accordance with FA, and that Russian suppresses inner case morphology in accordance with the One-Suffix Rule. Note now the following curious fact: were it not for the movement requirements of D that preserve primeval genitive in paucal and QUANT constructions, and were it not for the timing of phasal Spell-Out that insulates adnominals from the effects of DNOM morphology assigned in the higher DP, the language would offer *no sign whatsoever* that nouns have anything at all to do with genitive case. All evidence that a noun is primevally genitive and all evidence that it may assign genitive morphology would be obliterated by the assignment of DNOM by the D that selects the noun's maximal projection as a complement. Though these considerations do not argue in favor of either the overall proposal or the specific analyses of Russian that have been presented here, they do teach us that there is probably no simpler variant of the overall approach that might dispense with the auxiliary proposals, while still meeting the challenge of the facts.

For these reasons, I believe that the proposals defended here support the high-level, independently desirable conclusions sketched in chapter 2. The special case categories that have been considered indispensable in previous descriptions of languages like Russian may indeed reduce to independent categories of the syntax. I have proposed that the major case categories nominative, genitive, accusative, and oblique are simply the *parts of speech* D, N, V, and P—and that a lexical item that assigns a particular type of case morphology is simply copying a version of its own part-of-speech features. If my arguments in favor of this proposal are correct, we have to a significant extent eliminated the middleman—always a step forward.

Appendix 1

Nominative Plural Adjectives in Paucal Constructions

When an adjective modifies a feminine noun in a paucal construction, contemporary speakers of Russian tolerate two distinct patterns of case morphology on the adjective. The adjective may be genitive plural, just as it is when the noun belongs to the masculine or neuter gender. This is the pattern discussed in the body of the monograph and predicted by its proposals. Alternatively, however, the adjective may be *nominative* plural, which the analysis in the body of the monograph does not predict. Both alternatives are robustly attested with feminine nouns, but the unexplained nominative plural option for the adjective is several times more common than the predicted genitive plural (Suprun 1959, 73; Corbett 1993, 26; Pereltsvaig 2010), so it cannot be ignored.[1]

Though it is clear that the nominative variant is not predicted, it is not clear precisely how the problem should be characterized. At issue is a question seldom raised by either traditional or generative grammarians in this context: what morphology does the feminine *noun* bear when used with a nominative plural adjective? This question arises because the genitive nonplural (singular and numberless) form of feminine nouns in Russian is almost always syncretic with the nominative plural, as can be seen in (143a–b), which exemplify the two patterns found in paucal constructions with a feminine noun of declension class 2. (Feminine nouns of declension class 3 show the same syncretism.)

(143) **Case options in paucal constructions with feminine N (nominative environment)**

    a. dv-e   krasiv-yx   lamp-y
        TWO-F.NOM   beautiful-GEN.PL   lamp-GEN.SG°/NOM.PL

    b. dv-e   krasiv-ye   lamp-y
        TWO-F.NOM   beautiful-NOM.PL   lamp-GEN.SG°/NOM.PL

Though it is commonly assumed that the noun in both patterns is nonplural and genitive, it is also conceivable that the noun found with the nominative plural adjective in constructions like (143b) is actually *plural* and *nominative*, like the adjective that modifies it. If so, the variant in (143b) could now be described as an instance of the *homogeneous* pattern: in our terms, plural DNOM morphology assigned by D to all the elements of NP.

A puzzle would still remain, of course. What permits feminine nominal phrases to display a homogeneous pattern in environments where nonfeminines disallow it? On the other hand, a DP in which every element is nominative plural is a less exotic puzzle in the context of the current proposals than one in which the noun is genitive nonplural and the adjective is nominative plural. There is at least a pigeonhole made available by the theory, into which we can fit a nominative plural analysis of the noun in (143b). This is the same pigeonhole into which we fit the agreeing quantifiers discussed in section 6.2. We might thus stipulate the following:

(144) **QUANT-to-D movement optionality**
       QUANT-to-D movement is optional in a feminine nominal phrase if NBR has moved to QUANT.[2]

The optional application of QUANT-to-D movement will yield the pattern in (143a) (familiar from nonfeminine nominals), while the option of nonmovement will yield the novel pattern in (143b), on the assumption that the noun here is nominative plural.[3]

An interesting pattern of verbal agreement uncovered by Suprun (1959, 76–77) and explored further by Corbett (2006, 196–197) provides an argument in favor of this proposal: in particular, that QUANT-to-D movement is absent from examples like (143b) and that such examples do indeed instantiate the homogeneous pattern. When the highest argument of a clause is a quantified nominal of the sort that we have analyzed as showing QUANT-to-D movement, the finite verb shows a much-studied alternation between plural and default (neuter singular) agreement on the finite verb. Crucially, the uniformly homogeneous quantified nominals discussed in section 6.2—in which QUANT does not move to D—do not participate in this alternation. When such nominals are the highest argument in their clause, agreement on the finite verb must be plural.

(145) **Verb agreement alternation with quantified nominal in which QUANT moves to D (yielding a heterogeneous nominal)**

a. Na   stole   leža-l-o   pjat'-ʙ   bol'š-ix
   on   table.LOC.SG   lie-PST-N.SG   five-NOM   large-GEN.PL
   predmet-ov.
   object-GEN.PL

b. Na   stole   leža-l-i   pjat'-ь   bol'š-ix
   on   table.LOC.SG   lie-PST-PL   five-NOM   large-GEN.PL
   predmet-ov.
   object-GEN.PL
   'On the table were lying five large objects.'

(146) **No verb agreement alternation with quantified nominal in which QUANT does *not* move to D (yielding a homogeneous nominal)**

a. *Na   stole   leža-l-o   mnog-ie   bol'š-ie
   on   table-LOC.SG   lie-PST-N.SG many-NOM   large-NOM.PL
   predmet-y.
   object-NOM.PL

b. Na   stole   leža-l-i   mnog-ie   bol'š-ie
   on   table-LOC.SG   lie-PST-PL   many-NOM   large-NOM.PL
   predmet-y.
   object-NOM.PL
   'On the table were lying many large objects.'

When the highest argument is a feminine nominal that contains a paucal and a modifying adjective bearing *genitive plural* morphology, as in (143a), both plural and default singular agreement on the verb are possible, just as in (145), as shown in (147). Suprun and Corbett observe, however, that if the modifying adjective in such a sentence bears *nominative plural* instead, the alternation disappears. Only plural agreement is possible on the finite verb, as shown in (148).[4]

(147) **Verb agreement alternation with a feminine paucal nominal and *genitive plural* adjective (pattern (143a))**

a. Na   stole   leža-l-o   dv-e   bol'š-ix
   on   table-LOC.SG   lie-PST-N.SG two-F.NOM large-GEN.PL
   knig-i.
   book-GEN.SG°

b. Na   stole   leža-l-i   dv-e   bol'š-ix
   on   table-LOC.SG   lie-PST-PL   two-F.NOM large-GEN.PL
   knig-i.
   book-GEN.SG°
   'On the table were lying two large books.'

(148) **No verb agreement alternation with a feminine paucal nominal and *nominative* plural adjective (pattern (143b))**

a. *Na   stole   leža-l-o   dv-e   bol'š-ie
   on   table-LOC.SG   lie-PST-N.SG   two-F.NOM   large-NOM.PL
   knig-i.
   book-GEN.SG°/NOM.PL

b. Na   stole   leža-l-i   dv-e   bol'š-ie
   on   table-LOC.SG   lie-PST-PL   two-F.NOM   large-NOM.PL
   knig-i.
   book-GEN.SG°/NOM.PL

((147)–(148) adapted from Corbett 2006, 196–197 exx. (42)–(45))

In this respect, the paucal nominal in (148) behaves exactly like the corresponding quantified nominal in (146). If (144) is correct, and QUANT does not have to move to D in a feminine paucal nominal, we may attribute the impossibility of default verbal agreement to the same factor in both cases: the absence of QUANT in D. The same factor predicts that we will see the same homogeneous morphological pattern within the noun phrase. This prediction too is confirmed—so long as we can assume that the noun bears nominative plural morphology, not the homophonous genitive singular morphology that it bears when the adjective is genitive plural.

But can we actually make this assumption? Unfortunately, to the extent that it is possible to independently determine whether the feminine noun in paucal constructions like (143b) is nominative plural or genitive nonplural, the evidence is annoyingly equivocal. What we need to examine are situations in which the two forms can be distinguished—for example, situations in which they are not syncretic. There are two such situations.

In the first of these cases, we find some possible support for the nominative plural analysis. Surnames formed with the suffix -*in* or -*ov* such as *Puškina* or *Ivanova* show what is traditionally called a "mixed" declension pattern. When nominative and accusative, they bear the case suffixes typical of feminine nouns, but in other case forms (including the genitive), they bear the suffixes typical of agreeing elements such as adjectives, determiners, and agreeing quantifiers. As a consequence, the genitive nonplural and the plural nominative forms of these surnames are distinct (*Ivanov-oj* vs. *Ivanov-y*, respectively). As noted by Franks (1994, 600 n. 3; 1995, 52) and by Isakadze (1998, 54), in a paucal construction in a nominative environment, we find the unambiguously nominative plural form.[5]

(149) **Nominative plural of feminine surname in paucal constructions**
V   našem   klasse   učilis'   dv-e   Ivanov-y.
in   our   class   study.PST.PL   two-F.NOM   Ivanova-NOM.PL
'In our class there were two Ivanovas.'
(Isakadze 1998, 54 ex. (6))

While this might seem like a strong argument in favor of the proposal made here concerning (143b), there is another possible analysis that removes this support. It is possible that surnames in -*in* and -*ov* are actually adjectives, perhaps modifying a null noun. If so, the nominative plural morphology in (149) becomes simply another case of the puzzle with which this appendix began, and it tells us nothing special about the case of nouns. Since there are indeed other common surname types whose morphology is entirely adjectival (e.g., *Stravinskij*, fem. *Stravinskaja*), this possibility cannot be excluded in principle.[6] A possible argument against this counterproposal might be sought in additional data discussed by Isakadze. She marks as unacceptable the *genitive plural* form (*Ivanov-yx*) that should be available as an alternative to the nominative plural in (149) if the surname is an adjective (and is correctly predicted to be unavailable if the surname is a noun). Unfortunately, there is a counterargument to the counterargument: the genitive nonplural form that should be available as an alternative if the surname is indeed a noun (*Ivanov-oj*) is also impossible, as Franks notes. (Furthermore, the genitive plural form disallowed by Isakadze is not unknown in actual use, as a Google search reveals.) Consequently, (149) cannot be taken as a decisive argument in favor of the nominative plural analysis of the noun in constructions like (143b).

The other circumstance relevant to the status of the noun in (143b) concerns several groups of feminine nouns whose genitive nonplural and nominative plural forms are segmentally syncretic, but differ in stress: for example, *gor-ý/ gór-y* 'mountain-GEN.SG/NOM.PL'. (Some of these nouns shift stress only in the nominative and accusative forms of the plural, while others shift stress in other plural forms as well—a distinction not relevant to our discussion.) If the noun in constructions like (143b) is nominative, we might expect the stress pattern of the plural. If instead the traditional description is correct, and the noun is genitive, we would expect the stress pattern of the nonplural.

In fact, it is reported in the literature that speakers *avoid* such constructions. In particular, the use of a nominative plural adjective is repeatedly cited as dispreferred in paucal constructions where stress would otherwise disambiguate between nominative plural and genitive nonplural forms of the noun—with speakers resorting instead to the genitive plural variant (Crockett 1976, 341, citing Galkina-Fedoruk 1964, 365, and Kozyreva and Khmelevskaja 1982, 341; Rappaport 2002, 340; Koroleva 2005).[7] Furthermore, in nominal phrases without adjectives, the only possible stress pattern available for such nouns is the one associated with the genitive nonplural—that is, the form we expect if QUANT-to-D movement does apply. It is as if the language itself requires that the status of the noun in constructions like (143b) remain ambiguous between the two distinct case/number possibilities.[8]

Though I believe the proposal sketched in this appendix has not been falsified, and is in fact supported by Suprun's and Corbett's observation concerning verbal agreement, the issue is not settled. The correct analysis of the pattern in (143b) remains open.

Finally, note that the nineteenth-century pattern in which even masculine nouns could optionally cooccur with nominative plural adjectives is not explained by any variant of (144), since the genitive singular and nominative plural are not syncretic (at least for the vast majority of such nouns). As is often noted, the modern Russian use of the genitive singular in the paucal construction is probably the diachronic heir to the Old Russian nominative dual, which was uniformly syncretic with the genitive singular. Though I argued in section 8.4 against the proposal advanced by several researchers that the noun in a contemporary Russian paucal construction is nominative and belongs to a special "paucal number," it is possible that this is precisely the correct analysis of the earlier variant in which a nominative [−SINGULAR] adjective cooccurs with a noun bearing what looks like genitive singular morphology. I will leave this matter open as well.

Appendix 2

A Defectivity Puzzle: The Numeral-Classifier Construction

The Russian *numeral-classifier* construction investigated by Sussex (1976) and Yadroff (1999) can be viewed as an adnominal genitive construction that conforms to the proposals of this monograph, but with a slightly different profile due to interfering factors. One of these facts poses a puzzle for the analyses proposed in the main text.

Examples (150) and (151) show this construction in its most straightforward form, though not all speakers find this version of the construction natural.[1] Syntactically, these examples look like normal nominals containing an adnominal genitive (the bracketed phrase) and a numeral or paucal that has moved to D. The head noun in constructions featuring this type of adnominal, however, functions semantically as a classifier and must be drawn from a class limited for most contemporary speakers to the two nouns shown: *štuka* 'unit' for inanimates and *čelovek* 'person' for humans (but see Yadroff 1999, 91 n. 9, for some stylistically marked alternatives).

(150) **Numeral-classifier construction with classifier *štuka* 'unit'**

    a. pjat'-ь   štuk-ъ   [starinn-yx   knig-ъ]
        five-NOM   unit-GEN.PL   antique-GEN.PL   book-GEN.PL
        'five antique books'
        (Yadroff 1999, 109)

    b. dv-e   štuk-i   [starinn-yx   knig-ъ]
        two-F.NOM   unit-GEN.SG°   antique-GEN.PL   book-GEN.PL
        'two antique books'

(151) **Numeral-classifier construction with classifier *čelovek* 'person'**

    a. desjat'   čelovek-ъ   [naš-ix   oficer-ov]

       ten   person-GEN.PL   our-GEN.PL officer-GEN.PL

       'ten officers of ours'

    b. tri   čelovek-a   [naš-ix   oficer-ov]

       three-NOM   person-GEN.SG° our-GEN.PL officer-GEN.PL

       'three officers of ours'

       (Yadroff 1999, 146)

Yadroff shows that despite appearances, the classifier in these constructions is not a normal noun. (He assigns it to a category that he calls MEASURE.) In particular, it may not be modified by an adjective and must cooccur with a numeral or paucal (pp. 151–153). Crucially, it is also incapable of bearing (what we would call) POBL. This means that while the variant of (152) in which POBL has been assigned across a DP phase boundary is impossible for reasons explained by the proposal in the text, the variant in which the adnominal retains NGEN morphology is also impossible.

(152) **Classifier construction incompatible with POBL**

    *(k)   pjat-i   štuk-am   [starinn-ym   knig-am]   /

    (to)   five-DAT unit-DAT.PL antique-DAT.PL book-DAT.PL /

    *[starinn-yx   knig-ъ]

    antique-GEN.PL book-GEN.PL

In the absence of a principled explanation for this behavior, we might appeal to an independent notion of *defectivity* that can filter out the morphological results of otherwise legal applications of FA. Some QUANT elements have similar properties: for example, *malo* 'few', which also lacks POBL forms. It is not obvious that this is the right move, however. Morphological defectivity is commonly an idiosyncrasy of individual lexical items (such as *malo* among the QUANT elements). The defectivity relevant here, however, appears to be a property of an entire class of elements, as we can see by examining some particularly ingenious observations from Yadroff 1999.

The versions of (150)–(151) that are by far the most common (and most acceptable to speakers) involve an additional process of *Approximative Inversion*, which reverses the linear order of classifier and numeral, with the semantic effect of approximation.

(153) **Approximative inversion construction with classifier**

    štuk-ъ   pjat'-ь   [starinn-yx   knig-ъ]

    unit-GEN.PL five-NOM antique-GEN.PL book-GEN.PL

    'five or so antique books', 'some five antique books'

We may analyze this as movement of the classifier to D *before* QUANT-to-D movement takes place. DNOM is not assigned to the classifier by D because its movement requirements have not yet been satisfied, by the same logic that helped explain the case pattern in the "modified cardinal construction" in (66). Why this movement correlates with approximative semantics, however, is a mystery that has not been solved; nor can I explain why (153) is more common or acceptable than its nonapproximative counterparts in (150) and (151).

Crucially, approximative inversion is also possible in nominals that have no obvious classifier, such as (154).

(154) **Approximative inversion without overt classifier**

    knig-ъ   pjat'-ь

    book-GEN.PL   five-NOM

    'about five books', 'some five books'

Yadroff points out, however, that the noun in constructions like (154) shares the special properties that hold of the special classifier words *štuka* and *čelovek* in (150), (151), and (153) (see also Mel'čuk 1985, 147ff.; Franks 1994, 1995, 165ff.). First, it may not be modified by an adjective: adding *starinn-yx* 'antique-GEN.PL' anywhere in (154) renders the example unacceptable. Crucially, the construction in (154) is also excluded from POBL environments.[2]

(155) **Approximative inversion without overt classifier incompatible with POBL**

    *(k)   knig-am   pjat-i

    (to)   book-DAT.PL   five-DAT

    'to about five books'

Yadroff proposes that approximative inversion constructions like (154) are classifier constructions like (153), contrary to appearances. He argues that in the absence of an adnominal (which is optional in all classifier constructions, including the examples presented above), ordinary nouns may be coerced into the classifier class. If a noun coerced into the classifier class inherits an inability to bear POBL morphology, it is likely that we are not dealing with simple defectivity (an idiosyncratic property of individual lexical items); rather, we are dealing with some deeper factor that creates a conflict between oblique environments and classifiers.[3] The existence of such a factor comes as a surprise in the context of the proposals presented in this monograph. Yadroff's discoveries thus pose an interesting unsolved problem for the analysis.

Appendix 3

A South Slavic Argument by Horvath (2011) That "You Are What You Assign" Holds of Prepositions

In chapter 2, I introduced the idea that case morphology is nothing more than the copying of part-of-speech features, with particular reference to the proposal that since nouns assign genitive morphology, they therefore must be born genitive (i.e., "you are what you assign"). Throughout the monograph, I put this proposal to the test for nouns, by arguing that the distribution of genitive morphology on nouns can be explained if some of this morphology represents the genitive that the nouns are born with (while other instances of genitive represent morphology assigned by other nouns). The existence of visibly genitive contrasting with visibly nongenitive nouns provided hooks with which to test this proposal.

At the same time, I noted that it is particularly hard to give empirical teeth to this proposal for uninflected, monomorphemic words such as prepositions. As I remarked in chapter 2, "It is hard to find empirical predictions that can test such proposals—for example, that a dative-assigning preposition like Russian *k* 'to' assigns PDAT to its complement because the preposition itself belongs to the category PDAT." Nothing in this monograph has remedied this particular gap.

This task might be hard—but not necessarily impossible, if a proposal by Horvath (2011) is correct. Horvath presents an analysis of contrasts from Bosnian/Croatian/Serbian (BCS) discussed by Wechsler and Zlatić (2001) that appears to provide a direct argument that prepositions and the cases they assign

I am extremely grateful to Julia Horvath for the argument summarized here, and for further discussion. I also thank Liudmila Nikolaeva, Natalia Ivlieva, Alexander Podobryaev, Igor Yanovich, and especially Yakov Testelets and Irina Mikaelian, for discussion of the Russian data and related issues.

are in fact treated as tokens of the same set of features. The contrasts concern a class of indeclinable feminine nouns. These nouns (mostly borrowings) fail to show the normal -*a* suffix in the nominative and are therefore invariant in form across the various cases. Examples include foreign female proper names such as *Miki* or *Džejn* as well as the noun *lejdi*. These indeclinable nouns may be used as nominative and accusative arguments of verbs, but are excluded in positions where the main verb requires a dative or instrumental argument. (The situation with genitive is more complex, in ways I will not discuss here.)

(156) ***Indeclinable *Miki* (vs. declinable *Larisa*) as oblique object of V (BCS)**

    a. **Diviti se *'admire' requires dative***

        Divim   se   Laris-i   / *Miki.

        admire.1SG   REFL   Larisa-DAT   / Miki

        'I admire Larisa / Miki.'

    b. **Ponositi se *'be proud of' requires instrumental***

        Ponosim   se   Laris-om   / *Miki.

        be.proud.1SG REFL   Larisa-INSTR   / Miki

        'I am proud of Larisa / Miki.'

    c. ***Passive agent phrase appears in instrumental***

        Oduševljena   sam   Laris-om   / *Miki.

        impressed.F.SG AUX.1SG   Larisa-INSTR   / Miki

        'I am impressed by Larisa / Miki.'

Crucially, this generalization has two key exceptions, discussed by Wechsler and Zlatić. First, these indeclinable nouns are acceptable as complements to an *overt* preposition that requires dative or instrumental. (The parenthesized adjectives are present to provide minimal pairs for the next set of examples.)

(157) **Indeclinable *Miki* acceptable as oblique object of P (BCS)**

    a. ***The preposition* prema *'toward' assigns dative***

        On   je   trcao   prema   (lep-oj)   Miki.

        he   AUX.3SG ran   toward   beautiful-F.DAT.SG Miki

        'He ran toward (beautiful) Miki.'

    b. ***The preposition* sa *'with' assigns instrumental***

        Dolazim   sa   (moj-om)   Miki.

        come.1SG   with   my-INSTR.SG   Miki

        'I am coming with (my) Miki.'

    c. ***The preposition* o *'about' assigns locative case***

        Razgovarali   smo   o   (moj-oj)   Miki.

        talk.PST.PL   AUX.1PL about   my-F.LOC.SG   Miki

        'We talked about (my) Miki.'

Second, these nouns may appear with a verb that requires dative or instrumental case so long as it is modified by an adjective or other agreeing adnominal that shows the required case morphology. If an adjective is added that is just as indeclinable as *Miki*—for example, the borrowing *šik* 'chic' in (158c)—the structure does not improve.[1]

(158) **Addition of an adjective with overt case morphology eliminates the effect in (156) (BCS)**

    a. Divim se   *(moj-oj)   Miki.
       admire-1SG REFL   my-F.DAT.SG Miki
       (cf. 156a)
       'I admire (my) Miki.'

    b. Oduševljena   sam   *(moj-om)   Miki.
       impressed.FEM.SG AUX.1SG my-F.INSTR.SG Miki
       (cf. 156c)
       'I am impressed by (my) Miki.'

    c. Divim   se   {*šik / OK lep-oj}   Miki.
       admire-1SG REFL   chic /   beautiful-F.DAT.SG Miki
       'I admire {chic / beautiful} Miki.'

Wechsler and Zlatić explain the adjectival exception, but not the prepositional exception, as a reflection of a constraint that requires dative or instrumental case to be morphologically realized somewhere within the nominal phrase. Horvath (2011) points out, however, that a slight alteration of Wechsler and Zlatić's proposal can also explain the prepositional exception if the proposal in chapter 2 concerning oblique case is correct.

Assume that apparent dative and instrumental nominal arguments of V are actually PPs whose head is null, as has been proposed throughout this monograph. Add to this the hypothesis just introduced that a preposition that assigns a particular oblique case POBL assigns that case because the *preposition itself is an instance of POBL*. As Horvath notes, if we alter Wechsler and Zlatić's constraint to require BCS POBL to be *morphologically realized somewhere within the domain in which it was assigned*, then the puzzle is eliminated. So long as the PP contains either a declinable noun, a declinable modifier or other adnominal, *or an overt preposition*, the constraint is satisfied. Only a PP that lacks all of these elements will violate it.

Russian indeclinable nouns are not subject to the constraint observed in BCS, but for some speakers, the same condition does apply to indeclinable multiword phrases (such as non-DP book titles), when they are used as arguments. For example, Testelets (2011) has observed that while (159a) is acceptable, where the main verb otherwise takes an accusative object, examples like

(159b), in which the main verb requires an object with instrumental case, are impossible. For some speakers, adding the instrumental-marked adjective in (159c) improves the structure, as does the use of an overt preposition in examples like (159d) (a widely shared judgment).

(159) **A Russian parallel to (156)–(158)**

a. *Indeclinable book title acceptable as argument of verb that assigns V_{ACC}*

Ja   čital   *Po kom zvonit kolokol.*   (ACC object required)
I   read   *For Whom the Bell Tolls*

b. *Verb 'admire' requires P_{INSTR} on its argument and disallows indeclinable book title as object ...*

??Ja   vosxiščajus'   *Po kom zvonit kolokol.*
I   admire   *For Whom the Bell Tolls*
                                                    (INSTR object required)

c. *... but improves with the addition of a declinable adjective*

? Ja   vosxiščajus'   zamečatel'n-ym
  I   admire   marvelous-INSTR
Po kom zvonit kolokol.
For Whom the Bell Tolls
'I admire the marvelous *For Whom the Bell Tolls*.'

d. *Preposition **nad** requires P_{INSTR} but allows indeclinable book title as object*

Pomnju,   kak   diko   rydala   nad
remember.1SG   how   wildly   cried.FEM.SG   over
Po kom zvonit kolokol.
For Whom the Bell Tolls
'I remember how wildly I cried over *For Whom the Bell Tolls*.'
(http://www.livelib.ru/selection/1565/comments, accessed March 12, 2012)

Thus, in a very limited domain, Russian too may provide a direct argument that "you are what you assign" holds of indeclinable elements such as prepositions.

Notes

1. A. M. Peškovskij's (1878–1933) remarkable, wonderful book *Russkij sintaksis v naučnom osveščenii* (*Russian Syntax in a Scientific Light*) remains to this day a source of insight into almost all the central problems of Russian grammar—except, perhaps, this one.

Chapter 1

1. The noun *stol* 'table' in (1) is masculine. Substituting a feminine head noun sometimes produces a different pattern, in which postpaucal adjectives show nominative rather than genitive morphology—though the pattern found with masculine nouns remains possible and is also common. The pattern that mirrors the masculine (genitive plural) is sometimes felt to be more colloquial, and is sometimes held to differ in meaning from the alternative pattern (which is considered the literary norm). I will ignore the alternative form of feminine examples throughout the body of the monograph, returning to the topic in appendix 2.

Likewise, a celebrated group of five nouns show a stress pattern when used with paucals distinct from that found in other genitive environments. I discuss these nouns in section 8.4, but ignore the stress differences until that point.

2. A few preliminary remarks about other numerals and quantifiers may be useful at this point:

• Some nonnumeral quantifiers behave like the nonpaucal numerals. These are discussed in section 6.1.

• Additive compound numerals such as *dvadcat' pjat'* 'twenty-five' whose second component is a nonpaucal numeral show the same pattern as well. Additive compound numerals whose final component is a paucal, however, generally show the pattern of simplex *paucals*. In a nominative environment, a nominal containing *dvadcat' dva* 'twenty-two', for example, will show the same pattern of number and case as that seen with *dva* 'two' in (1b). Ionin and Matushansky (2006) argue that such examples actually involve NP coordination along the lines of *these last* [*twenty* (~~beautiful tables~~)] *and* [*two beautiful tables*]. They tentatively suggest that backward ellipsis applies as indicated to yield the observed form. Though their proposal raises some questions (including a few to which I return in note 10 of chapter 6 and note 5 of chapter 7), I will tentatively assume it for the remainder of the monograph.

• The numeral *odin* 'one' (and additive compound numerals ending in *odin*, such as *dvadcat' odin* 'twenty-one') differs in its behavior from all other numerals. I ignore *odin* for the time being, returning to its morphosyntax briefly in section 6.2.

3. The nonpaucal numerals themselves show the case morphology expected of a *singular* noun, rather than the case morphology characteristic of a plural. The *-i* suffix on *pjat-i* is thus the same as that found on dative *singular* nouns of the declension class 3. This fact will be important in chapter 7.

Chapter 2

1. The traditional list of Russian cases consists of *nominative* (NOM), *genitive* (GEN), *dative* (DAT), *accusative* (ACC), *instrumental* (INSTR), and *prepositional* (PREP)—plus, for some masculine nouns, a distinct *partitive* variant of genitive and a distinct *locative* variant of prepositional. There are three major declension classes (with some subclasses) and three genders (masculine, feminine, and neuter). This monograph follows the tradition in Russian linguistics that calls the (mostly feminine) declension class whose nominative suffix is *-a* "class 2." This corresponds, somewhat confusingly, to the "first declension" familiar from Latin and Greek traditional grammar (and some grammars of Russian as well).

2. Five masculine nouns show a different stress pattern in postpaucal position than in (other) genitive environments. This fact is sometimes invoked to argue that postpaucal nouns do not bear genuine genitive case at all. I will discuss these nouns, and argue that they do display genitive morphology, despite the stress difference, in section 8.4.

3. In theories like those advanced by Neidle (1988, 2–6) and Franks (1995, 41–55), cases such as "genitive" are not atomic categories, but matrices of distinctive features that cross-classify the various cases and characterize markedness relations among them. These features themselves, however, are just as sui generis as the traditional case categories, and function as middlemen between syntax and morphology in just the same way. They are therefore subject to the same criticisms. These approaches were, however, inspired by the proposals of Jakobson (1984a [orig. 1936], 1984b [orig. 1958]), who can be read as attempting to remedy some of the same flaws in the conventional view as those I have discussed here. Jakobson posited a feature system in which each case either bears a fixed *semantic* value or else stands in opposition to a case with fixed semantic value (i.e., signaling the absence of that value). His particular proposals have been sharply and effectively criticized on empirical grounds, however, by Neidle and by Franks (esp. pp. 43–44). (See also Pesetsky and Torrego 2001, 407 n. 17.)

4. The so-called prepositional and locative cases are mostly syncretic with each other, but are distinct for a small class of nouns. There are also partitive forms for some nouns, which I will not discuss here, and vocatives, which I will also not discuss.

5. The proposal will not depend on any particular feature theory for the parts of speech that are featurally distinguished. For the major lexical categories, we may assume the well-known two-feature system (±N, ±V) proposed by Chomsky and Lasnik (1977; but

cf. Baker 2003). I will make no explicit proposals concerning the featural decomposition of other categories discussed here, such as D.

6. This proposal may seem to contrast with more recent proposals according to which case morphology reflects a process of agreement. In section 4.3, I argue that agreement does play a role in the distribution of case morphology, but that this role can be distinguished from the role played by the assignment rule in (5). In section 7.2, I will also argue that Vergnaud's syntactic "Case theory" (often viewed today as part of the theory of agreement) is a system distinct from the system that assigns case morphology discussed in this monograph—no matter how much the technical side of FA may remind us of Vergnaud's and Chomsky's early proposals concerning "Case assignment." As I will note, my conclusions on this matter converge strikingly with proposals made by Schütze (1997, 2001) concerning "default case" and its relation to "Case theory."

7. Hard, but not impossible. See appendix 3 for a summary of an argument from Bosnian/Croatian/Serbian due to Horvath (2011), with an extension to Russian.

8. If Halle and Marantz (1994) are correct that the so-called theme vowel attached to the stem of the Russian verb is the verbalizer of a category-neutral root, then it is this vowel, in light of (4), that we should view as an instance of V$_{ACC}$.

9. The proposal advanced in this monograph is not compatible with Marantz's (1997) proposal that nominalizers and verbalizers are introduced syntactically outside a root-headed phrase that includes complements and modifiers. It will be crucial, for example, that when a complement merges with a head H, H is already categorized as a noun, verb, and so on—as in traditional approaches. The idea that nouns involve a categoriless root and a nominalizing morpheme (or that a verb contains the same root and a verbalizing morpheme, as entertained in note 8) is, of course, logically independent of the question of where the nominalization process takes place.

10. In section 7.2, I will also argue, in very similar fashion, that the category D is "born nominative" (which will turn out to be equivalent to Schütze's (1997, 2001) claim that nominative is a morphological default)—and for this reason assigns nominative to its syntactic dependents.

Chapter 3

1. Actually, in section 9.4 I will suggest that overt case stacking is found in some fairly dark corners of Russian morphosyntax; but apart from these possible instances, the generalization is absolute.

2. Since many case suffixes are single (surface) vowels, it might be thought that this effect is phonological: attributable to "Jakobson's rule," which reliably deletes a vowel before another vowel in inflectional contexts. Unfortunately, some case suffixes that are regularly suppressed by others end in a consonant (e.g., the adjectival genitive plural suffix -*yx*), so Jakobson's rule cannot be a general solution.

3. See Nevins and Bailyn 2008 for independent evidence for a phonologically zero (but underlyingly vocalic) genitive plural suffix in examples like (8d).

4. My use of the *yer* symbol will be inconsistent. I will use it when it is important to note the presence of a null case suffix, but will omit it otherwise (including in many places where a yer-minded phonologist would posit one). I will also silently replace ъ

(the "back yer") with the distinct symbol ь (the "front yer") after palatalized consonants—but only because the use of the former would unduly discomfort readers who know something about the language.

5. As Hale (1998, 202) points out, however, if the subject originates internal to vP, we might expect it to receive FUT morphology in its base position, contrary to the facts of Lardil. In section 7.2, I will argue that nominals receive morphology under FA only once they are fully licensed in the manner discussed there (i.e., once they receive "case" in the sense developed by Vergnaud (2006 [orig. 1976])). If this licensing either involves a category higher than the assigner of TFUT or occurs or else takes place after movement to subject position, the failure of FUT assignment to the subject can be explained. Hale notes that in the Australian language Pittapitta, FUT morphology does appear on the subject, and he speculates that the subject in Pittapitta (unlike its Lardil counterpart) might remain VP-internal on the surface.

6. Though the allomorph of ACC found here is segmentally null, Richards argues for its presence because it protects the final vowel of the INSTR suffix from an obligatory word-final deletion process that it would otherwise undergo.

7. My analysis of much of the Lardil data is heavily influenced by Richards's approach to the same phenomenon, which analyzes stacking in a manner fundamentally similar to the approach developed here—and even advances a comparison to certain properties of Russian case morphology. One major difference lies in the motivation for the deletion of case suffixes such as ACC in a FUT-marked nominal. Where I appeal to the One-Suffix Rule plus a set of Lardil-specific exceptions to explain which case morphemes do and do not delete under stacking, Richards appeals to a general rule deleting semantically meaningless morphemes like ACC (but not INSTR or GEN), a rule that has a phonologically detectable effect (nonpronunciation) only when it precedes Spell-Out to PF for the phase containing the morpheme. What is Lardil-specific on Richards's approach is the assignment of particular features to phasal categories that have the capacity to hasten or delay Spell-Out to PF. For example, it is the presence of a [CASE] feature on Lardil relative clauses that delays Spell-Out of the relative clause to a point past the assignment of ACC (so ACC is pronounced, despite later deletion), but before the assignment of FUT (so FUT is not pronounced, despite possible later assignment). To keep the discussion as clear as possible, I will not attempt a full comparison of my proposal with Richards's here, but I will discuss the interaction of case morphology with phasal Spell-Out in greater detail in chapters 8 and 9.

Chapter 4

1. With the inanimate nouns shown in (20), accusative environments behave exactly like nominative environments. I delay discussion of accusative until chapter 7. I will also limit the discussion to masculine nouns of the declension class seen in (20) (declension class 1), for reasons discussed in appendix 1.

2. See the discussion of (33) below for plural adjectival agreement with a conjunction of singular nominals.

3. This proposal resembles the suggestion tentatively entertained by Zaliznjak (1967, 46 n. 17) (who also cites precedents from Hungarian and Estonian numeral

constructions) that "in these circumstances, the meaning of plurality might be contained only in the numeral, while the noun only names the type of objects counted."

4. The proposed Russian dual, trial, and quadral thus have the properties of the Sanskrit dual, which could be used without an additional (overt) numeral to denote a set containing two individuals (on the crucial assumption that *dva*, *tri*, and *četyre* are not numerals)—and differs from the Slovenian dual, which "tends to be used only when the quantifiers 'two' or 'both' are explicitly stated in the context, and are replaced by the plural when this quantifier is unstated, even if a pair of referents are obviously implicit" (Priestly 1993, 440–441; cited in Corbett 2000, 43). I am grateful to Greville Corbett (personal communication) for clarification of these issues. In section 6.1, on the other hand, I will suggest that a null numeral is actually present when Russian dual, trial, or quadral is used, which might suggest that Russian is more like Slovenian than it might seem (or else that Sanskrit also boasted a null numeral in similar contexts).

Note also that the paucal *oba* 'both' must presumably be viewed as an instance of dual number that licenses a null 'all', since 'both' is 'all two'.

5. One possible objection to the present proposal is the fact that it posits freestanding instances of number that do not appear to have bound morpheme counterparts in other languages with number morphology. Though I posit a free-morpheme exponent of "quadral" number, for example, Corbett (2000, 26–30) suggests that genuine quadrals— that is, "a set of forms specifically for the quantity four"—are unattested, arguing that the few cases that have been argued to instantiate this possibility do not in fact show genuine quadral forms. Furthermore, in the context of the proposals developed here, we must probably view the paucal *pol* 'half' and the paucal uses of *četvert'* 'quarter' discussed by Mel'čuk (1985, 322ff.) as instances of fractional number specifications— with *poltora* 'one and a half' perhaps a portmanteau form of an additive complex numeral (cf. note 2 of chapter 1) whose second component is 'half' (though its etymology is actually 'half of the second'; Vasmer 1986, vol. 3, 319). Morphologically bound instances of fractional number also appear to be unattested.

I will not attempt to answer this objection, but will leave it as a concern for the future. If the present proposal is correct, Universal Grammar might indeed exclude quadral and fractional morphology, but crucially must not prevent a language from using a feature system for number that allows such values in principle. We might then speculate that it is precisely the fact that the Russian feature system countenances quadral and fractional number that requires it to have freestanding morphemes as exponents of these feature sets. Speculating further, one might imagine an implicational universal that requires the exponents of dual and trial number to be free rather than bound morphology, precisely because quadral number must be freestanding: "If a language has a freestanding number morpheme for quantity *n*, all morphemes for quantities less than *n* must be freestanding as well" (a possible elaboration of Greenberg's (1963) Universal 34: "No language has a trial number unless it has a dual. No language has a dual unless it has a plural"). Since I have not investigated these questions further, I will leave them for future research.

6. I believe that nothing in this monograph hinges on the precise internal organization of the subfeatures of [–SINGULAR] that yield dual, trial, and quadral number. For example, as Asya Pereltsvaig (personal communication) points out, they might all be

subfeatures of the category PAUCAL. See Harley and Ritter 2002 for an approach that could be extended to suit the needs of the present analysis.

7. The word order in (26b) is not completely impossible, but it requires strong focus on the adjective and is not compatible with a neutral information structure within the nominal. I will assume that the order in (26b) results from DP-internal focus movement of the adjective, of the sort discussed by Irurtzun and Madariaga (2010).

8. The proposal as stated requires that Russian nominal phrases are DPs, despite the general absence of overt determiners. This conflicts with Bošković's (2008, 2010) proposal that such phrases lack a DP projection in Russian and other Slavic languages (debated further by Pereltsvaig (2007b) and Bošković (2009)). As Željko Bošković (personal communication) points out, however, much of the discussion in this monograph could be reconstructed if what I call D were identified with some other element in the nominal functional sequence, while the direct analogue to D remained absent from Russian. I will not explore this possibility here, however.

9. A third approach, advanced by Chomsky (1995), accepts head movement at face value as a phenomenon, but attributes it to a "phonological" rule that applies outside the syntactic derivation (and therefore fails to feed semantic interpretation). Lechner (2006) and Hartman (2011) argue against this approach, demonstrating semantic effects associated with head movement.

10. See Wiland 2008 and 2009, chap. 2, for some strong additional arguments for the existence of head movement in the Slavic verbal system (specifically Polish).

11. See Pesetsky and Torrego 2001, 363, for a specific proposal, the Head Movement Generalization. Because it subsumes Travis's (1991) Head Movement Constraint, the Head Movement Generalization is incompatible with the head movement posited in this section, but it is compatible with the final form of the proposal as it will be developed in chapter 6.

12. It is important that the demonstrative be a specifier (or modifier) of D, rather than an instance of D itself; otherwise, we would not account for either its linear position or its case marking. Demonstratives may also modify N, in which case it appears to the right of D (here, to the right of the paucal) and bears NGEN morphology, as predicted.

(i) **Demonstrative modifying N**

dv-a	èt-ix	krasiv-yx	stol-a
two-M.NOM	these-GEN.PL	beautiful-GEN.PL	table-GEN.SG°

Mel'čuk (1980, 805 n. 9), commenting on a comparable example with a nonpaucal numeral, notes a semantic difference. When the demonstrative follows the numeral, the DP is indefinite ('some two of these beautiful tables'), with no implication that the set under discussion is maximal, while a DP in which the demonstrative precedes the numeral is definite.

13. Russian contains no null P that assigns prepositional case, which thus always depends on the presence of an overt preposition. As mentioned above, some nouns have a distinct locative case form, which has the same property (so locative case always cooccurs with an overt preposition).

Chapter 5

1. The exceptions are few. Approximately ten class 3 inanimates, which share an independent declensional peculiarity, are neuter; one class 3 noun, *put'* 'road', is masculine; diminutives present a few complications; and a few archaic words have unexpected gender. There are also indeclinable nouns, mostly foreign borrowings, which belong to no declension class. Their gender is also generally predictable (masculine or feminine if animate, neuter otherwise), with a few exceptions. I will not discuss these nouns here.

2. Some speakers have prescriptivist objections to any instance of feminine agreement with class 1 nouns (Crockett 1976, 93–94). Others allow feminine agreement on the verb, but not on an attributive adjective (Mel'čuk 1985, 475). There is social and regional variation, too, as well as a correlation with educational level (see Corbett 1983, 30–39, which cites a number of surveys). Nonetheless, the option is solidly attested in the contemporary language, and, as far as I can tell, speakers consistently detect the crucial contrast between the excluded pattern in (35c) and the alternatives exemplified by (35b) and (35d).

3. This contrast has been frequently noted. The 1970 Academy Grammar (Švedova 1970, 555, §1300.3) remarks that though generally "there is no strict rule for choosing the gender form" of nouns like *vrač* when they refer to a female individual, an exception is made for "circumstances in which the subject is accompanied by an agreeing word-form in the feminine gender.... In these circumstances the feminine form in the predicate is obligatory: *Naša direktor skazala* ['Our director said (lit. our.FEM director said.FEM)'], *Novaja sekretar' vsë pereputala* ['The new secretary mixed up everything (lit. new.FEM secretary everything mixed.up.FEM)']." Pereltsvaig (2006, 485 n. 39) annotates the patterns in both (35a) and (35d) with two question marks, but still reports a contrast with the pattern of (35c), to which she assigns an asterisk. Timberlake (2004, 164) describes the agreement pattern in (35a) as "oldest, formal," the pattern in (35b) as "newer, informal, now standard," and the pattern in (35d) as "newest, not normative"—but tags (35c) as "systematically outlawed."

4. This idea can be developed technically in several different ways. One possibility would build on the fact that any noun that (unambiguously) denotes a female human belongs to the feminine gender in Russian, and would extend this rule to phrases as well. Once Ж is merged—but not before, in the case of nouns like *vrač*—the resulting phrasal projection of N unambiguously denotes a female. Application of the regular rule will assign the resulting nominal projection to the feminine gender.

5. This contrast was noted by Crockett (1976, 114–115) (though described in slightly different terms). Crockett cites a number of independent sources for the data, in addition to the judgments of her own consultants. In my own experience, I have found that even speakers who are uncomfortable with some instances of feminine agreement with class 1 nouns (see note 2) report that feminine agreement on a nominative paucal is much worse.

6. Zaliznjak (1967, 71, 77) describes the distinct feminine form in the plural of 'both' as disappearing, but my consultants find these examples unexceptionable. Furthermore, while nonfeminine plural forms of 'both' with feminine nouns are robustly attested in

Web citations, an informal investigation suggests that they are significantly outnumbered by their feminine counterparts.

7. Complicating the picture, in the singular, it is impossible for a feminine adjective to modify a class 1 *vrač*-type noun in any case other than the nominative (Crockett 1976, 92 ex. (68b), 100).

(i) **Feminine adjective modifying *vrač*-type noun incompatible with nonnominative case**

My	govorili	s	nov-**ym**	/ *nov-**oj**	vrač-**ëm**.
we	spoke	with	new-**M.INSTR.SG**	/ new-**F.INSTR.SG**	doctor-**INSTR.SG**

'We spoke with the new (female) doctor.'

If D (the assigner of D$_{NOM}$) is unique among case morphology assigners in not bearing an unvalued gender feature (as claimed in the text), it will be the only assigner to assign a gender-neutral version of itself under FA in the environment of Ж. We might then attribute the unacceptability of feminine agreement with every other case to an incompatibility between the feminine features of the morphology that these assigners copy onto *vrač* (because they bear a gender feature valued by Ж) and the roster of cases suffixes available to a class 1 noun when it attempts to realize the case features assigned to it. If the lexicon contains no way to realize [+FEMININE, +SINGULAR] versions of P$_{OBL}$, V$_{ACC}$, or N$_{GEN}$ on a class 1 noun (because all its singular case suffixes are specified as masculine), examples like (i) will be excluded as instances of "realization failure." The nominative counterpart will be acceptable, because D$_{NOM}$ does not copy any gender of its own onto N. In the plural, I suggest in chapter 7 (rule (79)) that all stems are assigned to class 1, masculine, feminine, and neuter alike—reflecting the fact that no gender distinctions are made in the plural (and the fact that the accusative form of all animate nouns in the plural follows a pattern that is limited in the singular to class 1 nouns). This means that there are [+FEMININE, –SINGULAR] suffixes available to plural class 1 nouns, in contrast to the singular, thus accounting for the acceptability of examples like (49).

In this context, it is worth noting that one consultant did describe examples like (49) as sounding "odd," while noting a sharp contrast with the nominative counterpart in (45b).

Chapter 6

1. See chapter 1, note 2 for the syntax of additive compound numerals. "Superhigh" numerals such as *million*, *milliard* 'billion', and *trillion* have the syntax of normal nouns with a DP adnominal, rather than the syntax of a numeral. The properties of these adnominals are identical to those of other nouns, as discussed in chapter 8. *Tysjača* 'thousand' optionally behaves like a higher numeral or like a normal noun (Mel'čuk 1985, 289ff.; Timberlake 2004, 190–191). I will not discuss these numerals further.

2. As mentioned in chapter 1, note 3, the numeral *pjat'* (and many other Q$_{UANT}$ elements), though treated as plural by the syntax, bears case morphology otherwise typical of *singular* nouns (of declension class 3). Such elements are exceptions to the general rule (34) that otherwise dictates the choice of singular or plural case morphology on the basis of the number specification of the base. Q$_{UANT}$ elements like *pjat'*, though

plural, must therefore stipulate that their case morphology is singular. Note that we can be sure that *pjat'* is grammatically plural (i.e., [–SINGULAR]) because the higher elements such as the demonstratives and adjective 'last' seen in (58) and (59) obligatorily bear plural morphology.

3. As Bartosz Wiland (personal communication) has pointed out, both NBR-to-QUANT and QUANT-to-D movement violate a condition crucial to Cinque's (2005) account of word order typology within DP, restricting DP-internal movement to constituents that contain N (the head of the "extended projection" of DP). This observation might constitute an argument against either Cinque's proposal or the proposals made here. Alternatively, it might be profitable to explore other formulations of these proposals that could provide ways to reconcile them. For example, if we modify Cinque's proposal so that it is NBR rather than N whose movement is crucial, then NBR-to-QUANT movement will no longer constitute a counterexample to Cinque's proposals (so long as we allow NBR to be generated as a subcomponent of N when it is not a free morpheme, as in the Russian paucal constructions). The problem of QUANT-to-D movement remains (at least when NBR has not moved to QUANT)—but here the locality and string-vacuousness of the movement might turn out to be the factor that exempts it from Cinque's condition. I leave these issues as problems for future research.

4. When *mnogo* is used with a mass rather than a count noun (translating English 'much' rather than 'many'), the noun is singular, as expected: *mnogo vod-y* 'a lot of water-GEN.SG'.

Some mass nouns belonging to declension class 1 take a special "partitive" form of NGEN morphology in this environment: -*u* instead of the normal NGEN suffix -*a* found on class 1 nouns (*mnogo čaj-u* 'a lot of tea'). This form is not limited to particular syntactic environments, however. It is found not only in the environment of QUANT elements, but also in adnominal genitive constructions (see chapter 8) whose head denotes a unit of measure: for example, *stakan čaj-u* 'a cup of tea'. Consequently, we may view this partitive genitive as a semantically conditioned variant of NGEN.

The form is also found as a direct object in a construction with no overt QUANT or head noun: *nalit' čaj-u* 'to pour some tea' (cf. French *verser du thé* 'lit. pour of.the tea; pour some tea'). Here we might posit a null noun with the syntax of a QUANT element, since the partitive genitive is replaced by oblique morphology in POBL environments, as we would expect from a QUANT construction.

5. Mel'čuk (1985, 378) observes that these forms may not be used as the final component of an additive compound numeral (e.g., **dvadcat' dvoe* 'twenty-two'), a fact for which I cannot offer an explanation. Consequently, as Mel'čuk notes, there is an effability gap. Although for most numerals there is a way to say "*n x*," where *n* is a numeral and *x* is a *plurale tantum* noun (see note 7), this is impossible when *n* is a numeral greater than twenty whose final digit is 2, 3, or 4. For example, though it is possible to speak of two, five, or twenty-five 24-hour periods, there is no way to speak of twenty-*two* 24-hour periods.

6. Something similar is true of adjectives used without an overt noun, such as *časovoj* 'sentry' (lit. 'hour's-length', adj.), *bol'noj* 'sick person, patient' (lit. 'sick', adj.). These too generally demand the special numerals that I claim are overt instances of QUANT numerals, and disallow paucals. If there is a null noun in these constructions, the impossibility of a paucal might be attributable to the absence of a numberless use of the null noun.

Greville Corbett (personal communication) points out that examples of *dva mužčiny* are attested in the Russian National Corpus, and suggests that environments that include other numeral phrases facilitate its use (e.g., *dva mužčiny i četyre ženščiny* 'two men and four women'). I will leave this possibility as a loose end.

7. The reader may wonder how we can possibly know what the dative forms of these numerals look like, if they are always replaced by the combination of null Quant and a paucal. The answer is this: the special forms under discussion for 'two', 'three,' and 'four' belong to a series that continues into the higher numerals as well, which grammarians of Russian usually call the *collective numerals*. The collective form of *pjat'* 'five', for example, is *pjatero*. (Most members of the collective series higher than 'five' are formed by affixing *-ero* to the normal form. The collective variant of 'four', *četvero*, also contains this suffix, though the root is altered.)

The collective series as a whole (high numerals as well as low) is used in a variety of contexts, though speakers' judgments vary and are often subtle (see Timberlake 2004, 195–196, as well as Mel'čuk 1985, 376–405; Mel'čuk presents a complex picture of the facts to which this brief discussion will not do justice). Roughly speaking, the collectives are used to count humans (for some speakers, males only) identified as members of larger groups, when the utterance "focuses on the fact that the group exists" (Timberlake 2004, 196). For this reason, they are commonly used with nationality nouns such as *amerikanec* 'American (n.)' and "social role" nouns such as *student* 'student'—and to count the children in a family, when the focus is on the children as a group and not as individuals. They are also used obligatorily, as Mel'čuk (pp. 64, 380) notes, in nonanaphoric contexts where English would use a bare numeral in an argument position to denote a group of people, as in Mel'čuk's example *U samoj vody ležali pjatero / *pjat'* 'At the water's edge there were five (*collective* / **noncollective*) [people] lying around'.

Crucially, as Mel'čuk also notes (p. 385), the use of collective numerals with inanimate *pluralia tantum*, unlike the uses of collectives just described, is limited to the low numerals 'two', 'three', and 'four'. For example, if we replace 'two' with 'five' in (63), the noncollective form *pjat'* is robustly preferred over the collective *pjatero*, just as dative paucal *dvum* in (65) is preferred over its collective counterpart. This is so because the unforced use of numerals from the collective series is limited to humans (with the special semantics sketched above). Similarly, though more subtly, if we replace 'two' with 'five' in (64), the use of collective *pjatero* has the effect described above—that is, calling attention to the men as a larger group. The neutral version is the noncollective *pjat'*.

The picture given in the text is therefore correct as far as it goes: the "special" forms of low numerals are used when paucal constructions are unavailable for lexical-grammatical reasons. The picture is complicated by the independent use of the numeral series that includes these low numerals when quantifying over human individuals with particular semantic properties. When these factors are excluded, either by using inanimate nouns or by paying attention to the presence or absence of semantic restrictions, the relevance of these numerals to the present proposal emerges.

8. Mel'čuk (1985, 309ff.), Timberlake (2004, 197), and others note a semantic distinction between the homogeneous quantifiers in this group and their nonhomogeneous counterparts—though the details of the distinction remain somewhat unclear. Mel'čuk, for example, appears to suggest that the restriction on the quantification is understood

as old information in the homogeneous variant, yielding an interpretation that might be described as partitive: for example, *many of the tables*, rather than *many tables*. He also suggests that the restriction is more likely to be viewed as composed of individual parts in the homogeneous variant, and as an undifferentiated mass in the heterogeneous variant. I have not investigated these differences. Mel'čuk also notes that in case forms other than (what I would identify as) DNOM and PDAT, there is homophony between *mnogo/nemnogo* and *mnogie/nemnogie*, so the relevant semantic distinctions cannot be detected in other environments.

9. The paucal numerals of Polish behave similarly (except when associated with a masculine personal—that is, adult human—noun), showing a fully homogeneous pattern even in nominative environments

(i) **Polish paucals showing homogeneous pattern in nominative environment**
Dwaj   mili   chłopcy   śpią.
two.NOM   nice.NOM.PL   boy.NOM.PL   sleep.PRES.3PL
'Two nice boys are sleeping.'
(Rappaport 2003a, 132 ex. (23b))

For the syntax of numerals with masculine personal nominals, see chapter 7, note 3.

10. Additive complex numerals whose final component is *odin* show singular morphology on all NP-internal elements, including N and NP-internal adjectives. Agreeing elements that I have analyzed as merging with a projection of D, however, show plural agreement.

(i) **'Twenty-one' (nominative environment)**
  a. èt-i   poslednie   dvadcat'   odin-ъ
     these-NOM.PL   last-NOM.PL   twenty.NOM   one-M.NOM.SG
     stol-ъ
     table-NOM.SG
     'these last twenty-one tables'
  b. dvadcat'   odin-ъ   krasiv-yj   stol-ъ
     twenty.NOM   one-M.NOM.SG   beautiful-M.NOM.SG   table-NOM.SG
     'twenty-one beautiful tables'

(For unclear reasons, my consultants find comparable examples that contain both pre- and postnumeral adjectives unacceptable: for example, **èti poslednie dvadcat' odin krasivyj stol* 'these last twenty-one beautiful tables'. No alternative morphological pattern renders the example more acceptable, however.)

If we continue to adopt Ionin and Matushansky's (2006) proposal that additive complex numerals involve coordination and backward ellipsis, as discussed in chapter 1, note 2, and also analyze numerals as moved to D, then examples like (ia–b) must involve coordination at the D′ level: for example, [DP (*these last*) [D′ *twenty* (*beautiful*) *tables*)] *and* [D′ *one* (*beautiful*) *table*]]. 'Twenty' moves to D in the left-hand conjunct, while 'one' does not move to D in the right-hand conjunct. The adjective 'beautiful' in the right-hand conjunct modifies a singular noun, and it bears singular morphology, since its own NBR feature was valued [+SINGULAR] by agreement with N. The demonstrative and the D′-level adjective 'last' bear plural morphology because they modify a conjunction structure, resulting in the value [−SINGULAR] for their NBR features; see the discussion of (33) in chapter 4.

In an oblique environment, though the NBR feature of POBL will be valued [−SINGU-LAR], like the demonstrative and the D′-level adjective 'last' in (i), it is a singular version of oblique case morphology that will appear on N and on its modifying adjective. This is predicted by the convention for determining the number specification of case morphology given in (34) in chapter 4. Since N in the right-hand conjunct is lexically valued as [+SINGULAR] (not numberless, since this is not a paucal construction), the variant of POBL morphology that will appear on N is correspondingly [+SINGULAR]. The same choice is made for the modifying adjective, which receives the same [+SINGULAR] NBR value by agreement with N.

(ii) **'Twenty-one' (oblique environment)**

    (k)   èt-im   posledn-im   dvadcat-i   odn-omu

    (to) these-DAT.PL last-DAT.PL twenty-DAT one-M.DAT.SG

    krasiv-omu   stol-u

    beautiful-M.DAT.SG table-NOM.SG

    'to these last twenty-one beautiful tables'

When N is a *plurale tantum* such as *sutki* '24-hour period' (discussed in section 6.1), it is valued [−SINGULAR] in the lexicon, and *odin* within an additive compound numeral actually shows plural morphology.

(iii) **'Twenty-one' (nominative environment)**

    dvadcat'   odn-i   sutk-i

    twenty.NOM one-NOM.PL 24h-NOM.PL

    'twenty-one days'

Chapter 7

1. The alternative pattern discussed in appendix 1, in which the adjective is nominative plural, is also available in this environment (and is in fact more common, as discussed there).

2. In the interests of clarity, this formulation ignores the details of underlying phonology that allowed Halle and Matushansky (2006) to justify the conclusions in (78) in the first place. I will also omit from further discussion the idiosyncratic morphology of personal pronouns.

3. An empirically equivalent statement for Russian would be, "Otherwise, it is syncretic with DNOM." This version of the proposal would avoid the stipulation that certain assigned cases are not morphologically realized. On the other hand, the possibility that certain instances of FA do not result in realized morphology might explain puzzling patterns outside Russian. For example, in Polish, where the morphosyntax of nominals with higher numerals otherwise resembles Russian, a masculine personal higher-numeral nominal—in an environment that one would otherwise call nominative—shows NGEN morphology (Rappaport 2003a, 126). If Polish higher numerals move to D, like their Russian counterparts (with the same effect on the NP left behind as in Russian), we can account for the NGEN morphology on the numeral if there is simply no realization rule for DNOM for a masculine personal numeral.

4. *Tetrad'* 'notebook' (and *mat'* 'mother' in (82d)) is glossed as accusative (rather than nominative) because V<small>ACC</small> *has* been assigned to the DP that contains it (by (77a), since the DP is [+FEMININE] and not [−SINGULAR]), even though the morphological realization of ACC on a noun of this class is null (by (80c)). I am grateful to Greville Corbett for pointing out the usefulness of clarifying this point.

5. When a DP contains an additive compound numeral whose last element is a paucal, V<small>ACC</small> morphology on the paucal is described as highly disfavored (Mel'čuk 1980, 810 ex. (31); 1985, 200ff.; Timberlake 2004, 192 esp. n. 28) or "bookish" (Rappaport 2003b, 19). Instead, the paucal bears D<small>NOM</small> morphology, as if the object were inanimate, as shown in (i), an abridgment of Mel'čuk's example.

(i) **Animate object paucal in additive compound numeral treated as if inanimate**

Terroristy otpustili	[tridcat'	četyre/*cetyr-ëx	založnik-a].
terrorists released	thirty.NOM	four-NOM/*ACC=GEN	hostage-GEN.SG°

'The terrorists released thirty-four hostages.'

If we adopt Ionin and Matushansky's (2006) proposal for compound numerals (see chapter 1, note 2, and chapter 6, note 10), there is no obvious account for these facts, which I leave as an unsolved problem. Mel'čuk (1980, 810; 1985, 427) also notes that if one tries to add a form of *vse* 'all' to the object DP in (i), the result is ineffable. Neither the animate V<small>ACC</small> (= genitive) form *vse-x* nor the inanimate D<small>NOM</small> form *vse* is possible. I must leave this unexplained as well.

A similar unsolved puzzle arises from Mikaelian's (2013) observation (building on observations by Mel'čuk) that certain verbs (optionally) allow animate object paucal phrases to be treated as if they were inanimate, including atelic verbs of possession and perception, for example.

(ii) **Animate object paucal phrases treated as if inanimate**

a. Neploxo očen' imet' **tri žen-y**.
   three.NOM   wife-GEN°
   'It's very nice to have three wives.'
   (song from film *Prisoner of the Caucasus*)

b. Vojdja v dom, ja uvidel **tri čelovek-a** ...
   three.NOM   person-GEN°
   'Entering the house, I saw three people ...'
   (http://readr.ru/ales-adamovich%20karateli. html?page=35#ixzz1oeYiGkYw, accessed March 8, 2012)

6. If numerals like *pjat'* were grammatically singular—that is, genuine *singularia tantum* as Halle (1990, 170) proposes—they should license singular number agreement on agreeing elements inside DP (e.g., demonstratives) that probe into NP to determine their value for N<small>BR</small>. As Babby (1987, 102) and others have noted, this was in fact the norm in Old Russian, but it is not the case in the modern language, where the plural demonstrative seen in (2) is the only option.

7. Rappaport (2003b) cites examples of nonstandard usage from Krys'ko 1994, in which a paucal in an animate nominal fails to show the accusative form syncretic with the genitive seen in (83). Instead, it patterns with numerals like *pjat'* in (84) in showing a form identical with the nominative (and with the compound numerals discussed in

note 5 above). Since the actual case suffixes found on paucals are not completely identical to those found with plural nouns or adjectives in any case, we might attribute this usage to a nonstandard grammar in which paucals fail to undergo rule (79), which would otherwise assign them to declension class 1.

8. I owe to Halle (1990, 170) the idea that the absence of genitive-accusative syncretism for words like *pjat'* should be attributed to their declension class and the idiosyncratic fact that their case morphology is exclusively singular. I differ only on the small point that it is not membership in declension class 3 that is crucial to the absence of genitive-accusative syncretism, but rather failure to belong to class 1. This avoids an objection to Halle's approach by Rappaport (2003b), who notes correctly that numerals such as *sorok* 'forty', *devjanosto* 'ninety', and *sto* 'hundred' show the same pattern as *pjat'*, while not belonging to class 3. As it happens, these numerals all belong to aberrant declension classes of their own, otherwise unattested in Russian. Consequently, it is reasonable to exclude them from class 1.

Although my account rests on these two unexplained (and possibly unexplainable) facts, they are facts that are true *independently* of the issues under discussion here. This property of the proposal contrasts favorably, I believe, with alternatives such as those proposed by Babby (1987, 110–111) and Rappaport (2002, 339), who posit a special property of such numerals (absence of animacy features) whose sole consequence is to provide an explanation for (84).

Also relevant is the fact that the *collective numerals* such as *dvoe*, analyzed as "special QUANT forms" in section 6.1 (see chapter 6, note 7), do show genitive-accusative syncretism in animate DPs (Mel'čuk 1980). Except for an idiosyncratic DNOM suffix -*o*, their declension is that of plural agreeing elements such as adjectives, that is, class 1. The contrast with noncollective numerals in genitive-accusative syncretism is predicted.

9. Ora Matushansky (personal communication) notes that this entails that an adnominal DP (such as the possessors and complements to N discussed in chapter 8) is Vergnaud-licensed within NP; otherwise, it would not receive NGEN morphology when it merges with a projection of the host N. This is a necessary conclusion in any case, since the licensing of such a DP does not appear to depend on any element outside its NP host.

10. As pointed out in chapter 3, note 5, Lardil provides an independent argument for this proposal. In Lardil, unlike Russian, certain instances of Tense assign case morphology to the constituents of vP, but the subject is excluded. If the (future) subject DP is only licensed once it exits vP, the absence of tense morphology is explained.

11. Two of the three exceptions cited by Timberlake (*čerez* and *skvoz'*) mean 'through' and might lack a nonaccusative use for semantic reasons (since the goal of motion changes continuously as the path is traversed). The third exception, *pro* 'about', is nonspatial and is harder to explain away. I leave it as an unsolved problem.

12. Compare English *into* and *onto* in idiomatic uses such as *Mary is into syntax* 'Mary has positive feelings about syntax (and acts on these feelings)', *I'm onto you* 'I've figured out your hidden agenda'.

13. As discussed by Nesset (2004), when an event is situated with respect to a time interval that is both precisely bounded and at least the size of a week, *v* is normally used with a DP that bears PREP morphology, as in the left-hand column of (90) and

(92). ('Week' itself takes the preposition *na* 'on', but with the same PREP (or LOC) morphology on its object.) Nesset attributes this usage to the fact that such an interval is large enough to be treated as a 'container'—extending, to the temporal domain, the normal locational use of *v* and *na*—and he argues that temporal *v* with the accusative is a default, used whenever the container metaphor is inappropriate. I am grateful to Pavel Caha (personal communication) for bringing Nesset's work to my attention.

14. It is also possible that *prezidenty* is actually treated as an inanimate here, in which case its nominative morphology is not an exceptional property of the preposition, but a normal property of inanimate plural nouns, as discussed above. Some suggestive arguments to this effect are offered by Marelj and Matushansky (2010), building on work by Mel'čuk (1985, 461–482) and Franks and Pereltsvaig (2004).

15. As observed by Borik (1995, 29; cited in Harves 2003, 237), (96a–b) also contrast with (96c–d) and (97) in another respect, surprising under the suggested analysis. Only the kinds of distributive *po*-phrases that do not assign PDAT to their complement may function as the external argument (hence, the subject) of a transitive verb. We might speculate that the POBL property of *po* in (96a–b) is incompatible with satisfaction of the EPP property of T, and that this property is absent from the version of *po* that is allowed to select a DP containing a paucal or numeral—hence the retention of DNOM morphology. If we were to analyze these examples as DPs, we would of course have a simple explanation for their ability to function as subjects, but we would then have no obvious way of understanding why the higher VACC fails to affect the morphology of the paucal and accompanying noun.

The sensitivity of *po* to the presence or absence in D of a paucal or numeral (or more generally, QUANT) is perhaps connected to the well-known sensitivity of verbal number agreement to the same factor, to which I return briefly in appendix 1. As discussed in Pesetsky 1982, Corbett 1983, and many other works, default neuter singular subject agreement alternates with plural agreement on the finite verb (subject to a variety of syntactic and semantic conditions)—but only when the relevant DP contains a paucal, numeral, or other QUANT element in D (under the present analysis). The option is missing for other DPs in standard Russian.

Chapter 8

1. I will assume without further comment that phrasal possessors are merged as specifiers of N, not D, at least in the constructions under discussion. Pronominal possessors (e.g., *moj* 'my') and possessors formed from certain proper names and kinship terms (e.g., *mamin* 'mama's', *Mišin* 'Misha's') may be merged higher, since their behavior in paucal and QUANT constructions resembles the behavior of demonstratives and other pre-D elements.

Note that this theory of adnominal genitive requires that the various elements that merge between N and D do not head their own independent projections. There is, for example, no NBRP formed by the merger of NBR and N in a paucal construction, nor do adjectives project when they merge with the phrases that they modify. Though the idea that elements such as NBR project is often coupled with the idea that Universal Grammar requires such elements to be merged in a strict, cross-linguistically stable sequence, these ideas are separable (as far as I can tell). The somewhat "conservative" syntax supported by the analyses in this monograph is thus compatible, I believe, with the "cartographic" discoveries about the internal structure of nominals and clauses that have been made by Cinque (1999, 2005) and others.

2. As Nikolaeva (2007, 51) notes, the "genitive of quality" permits numerals only in expressions of age such as (99c), for unknown reasons.

3. Some nouns have distinct case forms within a normal adnominal and in the context of a higher numeral. This phenomenon might be seen as a counterexample to the proposal that both adnominals and numeral contexts display NGEN (and thus as a threat to the argument that nouns assign genitive because they are "born genitive"). These examples divide into two categories, neither of which constitutes a true counterexample, I believe.

The first category consists of the nouns *čelovek* 'person' and *god* 'year'. In an adnominal DP, these nouns show the expected genitive plural forms *ljud-ej* and *god-ov* (as in *načalo 90-yx godov* 'beginning of the '90s', lit. 'beginning of the ninetieth years'). (The stem *čelovek-* is replaced by the suppletive stem *ljud-* in the plural, so *ljud-ej* is indeed expected.) When in the context of a numeral and plural, however, we find *čelovek-ъ* and *let-ъ* instead (e.g., *pjat' čelovek* 'five people', and (99c)). (*Let-ъ* is otherwise the genitive plural of *leto* 'summer'.) In fact, however, one also finds these forms in the context of "counting words" that are not syntactically numerals, such as *kuča* 'a whole bunch of' (e.g., *kuča čelovek* 'a whole bunch of people'), which has the morphosyntax of a normal noun (though *kuča ljudej* is also possible). This fact suggests that it is the semantics of *counting*, rather than the syntax of numerals, that governs the special distribution of these forms.

The second category (which is productive) consists of measurement terms such as *kilogramm*, for which the expected genitive plural *kilogramm-ov* is commonly replaced in numeral contexts by *kilogramm-ъ* (e.g., *pjat' kilogramm* 'five kilos'). It is possible, however, that these special forms are not the genitive versions of normal nouns, but the genitive plural versions of homophonous *classifiers*—a category independently attested in Russian (Sussex 1976; Yadroff 1999) and discussed in detail in appendix 2. As noted there (following Yadroff), classifiers can be distinguished from normal nouns by their inability to support adjectival modification. This is also true of the special genitive forms found in numeral contexts. Thus, while *pjat'-ъ kilogramm-ъ* rather than *pjat'-ъ kilogramm-ov* is the normal way to express a weight of five kilograms, *kilogramm-ov* rather than *kilogramm-y* is used in the presence of a modifying adjective: *pjat'-ъ polnovesn-yx kilogramm-ov* (*kilogramm-ъ) 'five full-weight kilograms'. (As discussed in appendix 2, *čelovek-ъ* may also be used as a classifier, providing a second possible analysis of this form.)

4. The presence of PINSTR morphology on this and a variety of other adjectival and nominal predicates in Russian suggests the presence within the small clause of a null preposition that assigns this morphology, perhaps a counterpart to English predicative *as* in *I regard this lamp as beautiful*.

5. There exist other nouns of declension class 1 whose stress pattern is superficially similar to that of nouns like *nos* and *zub*, but which are irrelevant to our discussion. These nouns also show stem stress in the singular and suffix stress in the plural, but with one key difference: stem stress is retained in the nominative plural (*zúb-y* 'tooth-NOM.PL'). If Halle's (1997) theory of Russian accentuation is correct, these are nouns

whose stems are lexically unaccented, not nouns that show idiosyncratic number-dependent stress shift. The nominative plural is the only class 1 plural suffix that lacks a lexical accent. This places stress on the initial syllable by the general rules of the language.

6. Responding to a draft of the present monograph, Xiang et al. (2011) conducted an experimental investigation of a prediction that they believe distinguishes between the hypothesis that the noun bears a special paucal form in paucal constructions and this monograph's hypothesis that the noun is genitive. Results from a morphological accept-ability judgment task and a self-paced reading task show increased processing load for the noun in a paucal construction, compared to the same noun in construction with numerals such as 'one' and 'five'. Xiang et al. take this extra processing load to reflect a morphological ambiguity posited for the noun under the "special paucal form" hypothesis, but not under the hypothesis that the noun is genitive—and thus interpret their results as supporting the former hypothesis over the latter.

In fact, however, the same considerations that allow us to explain the difference in stress pattern between nouns like *rjad* in paucal constructions and such nouns in other genitive environments are applicable to Xiang et al.'s results as well. There is a featural ambiguity particular to the noun in a paucal construction in the present theory as well. It is not an ambiguity between paucal and genitive case, but rather an ambiguity between numberlessness and singular number. Xiang et al.'s results therefore do not actually distinguish the hypotheses as claimed, at least not straightforwardly.

7. Vasmer's etymological dictionary (Vasmer 1986 [orig. 1950–1958]) does suggest a diachronic connection between *kolo* of *okolo* and *koleso* 'wheel', and between the *sle* of *posle* and the root found in words for 'follow' and 'trace' (*sled*).

8. Conceivably this noun is overt in the preposition *v-ne* 'outside' (thus perhaps more literally: 'in the complement set of'), which also requires a genitive DP.

9. The complements of certain verbs such as *bojat'-sja* 'fear' show genitive morphol-ogy. As with apparent oblique complements, I will assume that these verbs actually take a PP complement, within which the DP object is assigned NGEN. This PP, in turn, will be a null counterpart of those discussed in this section, whatever the right analysis of such PPs may turn out to be.

Chapter 9

1. The adnominal adjective in (124) is presumably assigned NGEN by *acteur*. We may assume either that this has no realization in French, or that perhaps its realization is the adjective's suffixal morphology usually taken to show only gender and number. I leave this question open.

2. Were it not necessary to posit deletion of internal instances of prototype categories, it would be tempting to identify the piling up of prototypes under FA with the "case sequence" that Caha (2009) posits as the outer structural shell of nominals in languages of the Slavic group and elsewhere. The actual ordering of cases posited by Caha differs substantially (and indispensably), however, from the ordering that would be found in a variant of the present proposal that dispensed with the One-Prototype Rule, so the two proposals are not easily unifiable.

3. In the much-studied genitive-of-negation construction of Russian, an internal argument of V in a negative sentence bears genitive morphology under particular semantic conditions that are the topic of some debate. See Harves 2002, 32–91, for a survey of the research that this construction has sparked.

(i) **Genitive-of-negation construction**

    Ivan   ne   čital   [xoroš-ix   knig-ъ].
    Ivan.NOM   NEG   read.PST   good-GEN.PL   book-GEN.PL
    'Ivan hasn't read (any) good books.'

In the context of this monograph, genitive case on this nominal must clearly be attributed to an outside assigner of NGEN. The genitive of negation is not an instance of "primeval genitive"—since in a noun phrase that contains a paucal or QUANT element that moves to D, everything including the material in D bears genitive case, and N must be plural, just as in other instances of assigned genitive discussed in the text.

(ii) **Paucal nominal in genitive-of-negation construction**

    Ivan   ne   čital   [dvu-x   knig-ъ].
    Ivan.NOM   NEG   read.PST   two-GEN.PL   book-GEN.PL
    'Ivan hasn't read two books.'

One possibility might attribute assignment of NGEN to a silent nominal negative polarity item or minimizer. As it happens, the French genitive-of-negation construction includes just such an element in the form of *pas*—traditionally viewed as a negation marker, but also a nominal meaning 'step'.

(iii) **French genitive-of-negation construction**

    Jean   n'   a   pas   lu   de$_{N}$•   bons   livres.
    Jean   *ne* AUX   *pas* read.PCP   of   good.M.PL   book.PL
    'Jean hasn't read (any) good books.'
    (cf. Kayne 1981, 48ff.)

If at some point in the derivation, *pas* is a sister to the object nominal, the presence of *de* is explained. A parallel analysis for Russian will also explain the presence of NGEN morphology. I will not pursue these conjectures further here, and leave the matter for future investigation.

4. The same appears to be true of control complements, as discussed by Klokeid (1976, 225ff.) and Richards (2007, 2013), who claim that the controller assigns case morphology into the complement clause. Available examples make it difficult to argue for a precise analysis of these cases, so I will not discuss them further here.

5. In all relevant examples that I have examined, and a wide range of textual examples that Norvin Richards kindly examined on my behalf, the rightmost word in possessive phrases that show case stacking is the head noun of the possessive NP. Nominals in which this noun is not rightmost are attested. For example, a possessor may follow the possessee, though this is not the commonest order, and we have seen relative clauses following the NP that they modify. On which word do we find stacked cases in possessive DPs whose rightmost element is not the head noun of its NP? Unfortunately, I do not know.

6. The analysis would obviously be improved if the special Genitive Haplology Rule could be eliminated in favor of a unified account of all the circumstances in which possessors fail to receive stacked morphology. Unfortunately, the facts of genitive haplology are different from the other facts considered in this section in a way that appears to make a unified account impossible, since the structural configuration in which genitive stacking would arise is a configuration in which (phrase-level) stacking is possible (morphology assigned by the category with which the possessee has merged).

7. Interestingly, Corbett (1986, 1008) also notes that "there are also instances" of an alternative pattern to (140b), in which the dependent of the special-form possessor shows the same case and ϕ-feature morphology as the possessor itself.

(i) **Alternative Sorbian agreement pattern**

w	naš-**ej**	nan-ow-ej	chěž-i
in	our-**F.LOC.SG**	father-SUFFIX-F.LOC.SG	house-LOC.SG

(Corbett 1986, 1008 ex. (42))

Under the proposal advanced here, in this alternative pattern, Spell-Out has not frozen the adnominal possessive 'our father', permitting subsequent assignment of D$_{NOM}$ and P$_{LOC}$ to be realized at the word level, overwriting the morphology on 'our' that remains visible in (140b). This means that there is some possibility for variation in the timing of Spell-Out. The nature of this variation is an open question.

8. Other compound modifiers whose first component is in principle inflectable (including compounds whose first component is *odin* 'one') do not show identifiable genitive marking as paucals and numerals do—but in its place show a special morpheme, often *-o*, which one might also identify as a special genitive.

(i) **Special morpheme in compound modifiers**

a.	*Krasnoarmejskij rajon*	krasn-o	+	armej-sk-ij
	'Red Army region'	red-SUFFIX		army-SUFFIX-M.NOM.SG
b.	*Odnoètažnaja Amerika*	odn-o	+	ètaž-n-aja
	'One-Story America' (book title)	one-SUFFIX		story-SUFFIX-F.NOM.SG

Appendix 1

1. A nominative plural adjective was also possible with nonfeminine nouns in the nineteenth century and earlier, but has all but disappeared as an option in the modern language (as Corbett's (1993) survey of actual usage makes clear). I will return to this possibility below, but I ignore it for now.

2. This analysis depends crucially on the two-step proposal introduced in section 6.1, by which NBR moves first to QUANT, since paucals in feminine constructions like (143b) linearly precede nominative adjectives within NP, just like their counterparts in paucal constructions with genitive adjectives. This indicates clearly that even though they might not move to D, they do not remain in their base position either.

3. This treatment of the nominative plural pattern predicts that adjectival case should be uniform throughout the DP. In a relevant nominal with multiple adjectives, it should

be impossible for some to bear genitive plural morphology, while others bear nominative plural. This prediction is correct.

An observation by Corbett (1979, 6) suggests that this prediction, for some speakers at least, is also confirmed by the behavior of prequantifier adjectives in the modified cardinal construction discussed briefly in section 6.1. In the examples discussed there (which uniformly contained masculine nouns), these adjectives appeared with genitive plural morphology, which we attributed to an initial NP-internal position in which N assigned NGEN. With a feminine noun, Corbett reports that the case of the prequantifier adjective must match the case of any adjectives that appear NP-internally, which supports the claim that these adjectives originate NP-internally, as Corbett notes.

(i) **Prequantifier adjective must match case of other adjectives**

    a. ✓cel-ye   / *cel-yx   dv-e   svobodn-**ye**

        ✓whole-NOM.PL / *whole-GEN.PL two-F.NOM free-**NOM.PL**

        nedel-i

        week-GEN.SG°/NOM.PL

    b. *cel-ye   / ✓cel-yx   dv-e   svobodn-**yx**

        *whole-NOM.PL / ✓whole-GEN.PL two-F.NOM free-**GEN.PL**

        nedel-i

        week-GEN.SG°/NOM.PL

        'a whole two free weeks'

These judgments also conform to those of my consultants. Nonetheless, as Asya Pereltsvaig (personal communication) points out, the starred version of (ia) is in fact widely accepted by other speakers (as an Internet search easily confirms). This is not predicted by the conjunction of the suggested analysis of feminine nominative plural adjectives with paucals and the analysis of prequantifiers like *celyx* 'whole' suggested in section 6.1. I will leave this as an unsolved problem.

4. Corbett (2006, 196) notes that "speakers have varying preferences" among the patterns exemplified by (147a–b) and (148a). My consultants, for example, disprefer (147b) compared to (147a) and (148b). Corbett describes the contrast between all three of these examples and (148a), however, as "clear-cut," a judgment confirmed by my consultants as well.

5. Franks describes the observation differently, suggesting that what we find is just the nominal, rather than adjectival *genitive singular* form—that is, a deviation from the partly adjectival pattern of morphology otherwise typical of these surnames. Since the genitive singular of feminine nouns is syncretic with the nominative plural (fully syncretic, including stress, for these surnames), the alternative description given in the body of this monograph fits the facts just as well as Franks's description does.

6. The possessive forms discussed in section 9.4 strongly resemble these surnames in -*in* and -*ov*, and also have a "mixed declension." As Garde (1980, 207) notes, however, the declension of these possessive forms is not completely identical to that of the corresponding surnames, differing in the prepositional case form for masculine/neuter singular (-*e*, as in nominals, for surnames; -*om*, as in agreeing elements, for possessive adjectives).

7. Contradicting the judgments presented in the text, Pereltsvaig (2010) reports that 72% (62) of 82 speakers polled in an e-mail questionnaire preferred a nominative plural

over a genitive plural adjective in a paucal context with the stress-shifting noun *gora* 'mountain', roughly the same distribution found with other nouns in the same survey. Since her result concerns a single test item in a larger survey where the same questions were asked about many non-stress-shifting head nouns, it is possible that the responses for the stress-shifting noun were influenced by the judgments on other nouns. The written nature of the experiment may also have played a role.

8. Genitive singular and nominative plural are also syncretic for neuter nouns. In this connection, it might be of interest that Corbett's (1993, 26) corpus data (though not Suprun's (1959) survey cited by Corbett) suggest that a nominative plural adjective is marginally available to neuter nominals (occurring in 7% of relevant neuter nominals vs. 69% for feminine nominals), in contrast to masculines, for which it is unavailable (0%). If the contrast were stronger, it might justify revising (144) as "QUANT movement to D is optional whenever it brings about no phonological change in N," a generalization that would raise many interesting questions about the relation between syntactic processes and morphological realization.

Appendix 2

1. Though my consultants do not find these examples utterly impossible, they find them significantly worse than counterparts with approximative inversion such as (153). They also report that without approximative inversion, classifier constructions with paucal numerals such as (150b) and (151b) are noticeably less acceptable than corresponding examples with nonpaucals such as (150a) and (151a). I will offer no account of these contrasts.

2. As Franks (1995, 170) notes, when a DP is an object of a (seemingly) accusative-assigning preposition, the noun commonly precedes the preposition (as well as the numeral) in the approximative inversion construction. I will not attempt to explain this pattern here.

3. See Billings 1995 for similar constraints on a distinct approximative construction with an ACC-assigning use of the preposition *s* (here = 'approximately') (which could be analyzed along similar lines).

Appendix 3

1. To demonstrate this point, Wechsler and Zlatić use the indeclinable form *braon* 'brunette', a word that does not behave as an adjective for all speakers. I have substituted *šik* at the suggestion of Martina Gračanin-Yuksek (personal communication).

References

Note: The author is responsible for all English translations of Russian-language sources in this monograph.

Acquaviva, Paolo. 2008. *Lexical plurals: A morphosemantic approach*. Oxford: Oxford University Press.

Asarina, Alya. 2008. Gender and adjectives in numeral constructions in Russian. Ms., MIT. [http://web.mit.edu/alya/www/russian-gender.pdf]

Babby, Leonard H. 1985. Noun phrase internal case agreement in Russian. *Russian Linguistics* 9, 1–15.

Babby, Leonard H. 1987. Case, prequantifiers, and discontinuous agreement in Russian. *Natural Language and Linguistic Theory* 5, 91–138. [http://www.jstor.org/stable/4047576]

Bailyn, John Frederick. 2003. The case of Q. In Olga Arnaudova, ed., *Formal Approaches to Slavic Linguistics 12*, 1–36. Ann Arbor, Michigan: University of Michigan Press.

Baker, Mark C. 1988. Against reanalysis of heads. In Denise Fekete and Zofia Laubitz, eds., *McGill working papers in linguistics, special issue on comparative Germanic syntax*, 35–60. Montréal: McGill University.

Baker, Mark C. 2003. *Lexical categories: Verbs, nouns, and adjectives*. Cambridge: Cambridge University Press.

Baker, Mark C., and Chris Collins. 2006. Linkers and the internal structure of VP. *Natural Language and Linguistic Theory* 24, 307–354.

Billings, Loren. 1995. Approximation in Russian and the single-word constraint. Doctoral dissertation, Princeton University. [http://roa.rutgers.edu/files/876-1006/876-BILLINGS-0-0.PDF]

Borik, Olga. 1995. Sintaksičeskij priznak neakkuzativnosti glagola (na materiale russkogo jazyka). Master's thesis, Diplomnaja rabota. Department of Theoretical and Applied Linguistics, Moscow State University.

Bošković, Željko. 2008. What will you have, DP or NP? In *Proceedings of NELS 37*, 101–114. Amherst: University of Massachusetts, Graduate Linguistic Student Association.

Bošković, Željko. 2009. More on the no-DP analysis of article-less languages. *Studia Linguistica* 63, 187–203. [http://web2.uconn.edu/boskovic/papers/StudiaLing.Final.pdf]

Bošković, Željko. 2010. On NPs and clauses. Ms., University of Connecticut. [http://web2.uconn.edu/boskovic/papers/npclauses.pdf]

Burzio, Luigi. 1981. Intransitive verbs and Italian auxiliaries. Doctoral dissertation, MIT. [http://dspace.mit.edu/handle/1721.1/15849]

Burzio, Luigi. 1986. *Italian syntax: A government-binding approach.* Dordrecht: Reidel.

Caha, Pavel. 2009. The nanosyntax of case. Doctoral dissertation, University of Tromsø. [http://ling.auf.net/lingBuzz/000956]

Chomsky, Noam. 1965. *Aspects of the theory of syntax.* Cambridge, MA: MIT Press.

Chomsky, Noam. 1980. On binding. *Linguistic Inquiry* 11, 1–46. [http://www.jstor.org/stable/4178149]

Chomsky, Noam. 1981. *Lectures on government and binding.* Dordrecht: Foris.

Chomsky, Noam. 1995. Categories and transformations. In *The Minimalist Program*, 219–394. Cambridge, MA: MIT Press.

Chomsky, Noam. 2000. Minimalist inquiries. In Roger Martin, David Michaels, and Juan Uriagereka, eds., *Step by step: Essays on Minimalist syntax in honor of Howard Lasnik*, 89–156. Cambridge, MA: MIT Press.

Chomsky, Noam. 2001. Derivation by phase. In Michael Kenstowicz, ed., *Ken Hale: A life in language*, 1–52. Cambridge, MA: MIT Press. [http://cognet.mit.edu/library/books/view?isbn=0262112574]

Chomsky, Noam. 2004. Beyond explanatory adequacy. In Adriana Belletti, ed., *Structures and beyond: The cartography of syntactic structures, vol. 3*, 104–131. Oxford: Oxford University Press. First published as MIT Occasional Papers in Linguistics 20. Cambridge, MA: MIT, MIT Working Papers in Linguistics (2001).

Chomsky, Noam. 2008. On phases. In Robert Freidin, Carlos P. Otero, and Maria Luisa Zubizarreta, eds., *Foundational issues in linguistic theory: Essays in honor of Jean-Roger Vergnaud*, 133–166. Cambridge, MA: MIT Press.

Chomsky, Noam, and Howard Lasnik. 1977. Filters and control. *Linguistic Inquiry* 8, 425–504. [http://www.jstor.org/stable/4177996]

Chvany, Catherine V. 1975. *On the syntax of be-sentences in Russian.* Cambridge, MA: Slavica Publishers.

Cinque, Guglielmo. 1999. *Adverbs and functional heads: A cross-linguistic perspective.* Oxford: Oxford University Press.

Cinque, Guglielmo. 2005. Deriving Greenberg's Universal 20 and its exceptions. *Linguistic Inquiry* 36, 315–332.

Cinque, Guglielmo, and Luigi Rizzi, eds. 2010. *Mapping spatial PPs.* Oxford: Oxford University Press.

Collins, Chris. 2003. The internal structure of VP in Jul'hoansi and ǂhoan. *Studia Linguistica* 57, 1–25.

Corbett, Greville G. 1979. Adjective movement. *Nottingham Linguistic Circular* 8, 1–10.

Corbett, Greville G. 1983. *Hierarchies, targets, and controllers: Agreement patterns in Slavic.* London: Croom Helm.

Corbett, Greville G. 1986. Agreement: A partial specification, based on Slavonic data. *Linguistics* 24, 995–1023. [http://www.surrey.ac.uk/englishandlanguages/research/smg/files/Grevs%20Files/Agreement-1986.pdf]

Corbett, Greville G. 1987. The morphology/syntax interface: Evidence from possessive adjectives in Slavonic. *Language* 63, 299–345. [http://epubs.surrey.ac.uk/1332/1/fulltext.pdf]

Corbett, Greville G. 1993. The head of Russian numeral expressions. In Greville G. Corbett, Norman M. Fraser, and Scott McGlashan, eds., *Heads in grammatical theory*, 11–35. Cambridge: Cambridge University Press.

Corbett, Greville G. 2000. *Number*. Cambridge: Cambridge University Press.

Corbett, Greville G. 2006. *Agreement*. Cambridge: Cambridge University Press.

Corbett, Greville G. 2008. Determining morphosyntactic feature values: The case of case. In Greville G. Corbett and Michael Noonan, eds., *Case and grammatical relations: Studies in honor of Bernard Comrie*, 1–34. Amsterdam: John Benjamins.

Crockett, Dina B. 1976. *Agreement in contemporary standard Russian*. Cambridge, MA: Slavica Publishers.

Dikken, Marcel den. 2006. *Relators and linkers: The syntax of predication, predicate inversion, and copulas*. Cambridge, MA: MIT Press.

Dikken, Marcel den, and Pornsiri Singhapreecha. 2004. Complex noun phrases and linkers. *Syntax* 7, 1–54.

Emonds, Joseph E. 1987. The Invisible Category Principle. *Linguistic Inquiry* 18, 613–632. [http://www.jstor.org/stable/4178563]

Fleisher, Nicholas. 2006. Russian dative subjects, case, and control. Ms., University of California, Berkeley. [https://pantherfile.uwm.edu/fleishen/www/papers/Fleisher_RussianDatSubj.pdf]

Fox, Danny, and David Pesetsky. 2005. Cyclic linearization and syntactic structure. *Theoretical Linguistics* 31, 1–46. [DOI: 10.1515/thli.2005.31.1–2.1]

Franks, Steven. 1994. Parametric properties of numeral phrases in Slavic. *Natural Language and Linguistic Theory* 12, 597–674. [http://www.jstor.org/stable/4047869]

Franks, Steven. 1995. *Parameters of Slavic morphosyntax*. New York: Oxford University Press.

Franks, Steven, and Asya Pereltsvaig. 2004. Functional categories in the nominal domain. In Olga Arnaudova, Wayles Browne, Maria-Luisa Rivero, and Danijela Stojanovic, eds., *Formal Approaches to Slavic Linguistics 12: The Ottawa meeting*, 109–128. Ann Arbor, MI: Michigan Slavic Publications. [http://pubs.cogs.indiana.edu/pubspdf///36374/36374_Functionalcategoriesinnominal.pdf]

Freidin, Robert, and Leonard H. Babby. 1984. On the interaction of lexical and structural properties: Case structure in Russian. *Cornell Working Papers in Linguistics* 6, 71–105.

Galkina-Fedoruk, E. M. 1964. *Sovremennyj russkij jazyk: Čast'ii*. Moscow: Moscow State University.

Garde, Paul. 1980. *Grammaire russe*. Paris: Institut d'études slaves.

Greenberg, Joseph H. 1963. Some universals of grammar with particular reference to the order of meaningful elements. In Joseph Greenberg, ed., *Universals of language*, 40–70. Cambridge, MA: MIT Press.

Hale, Kenneth L. 1997. Remarks on Lardil phonology and morphology. In Ngakulmungan Kangka Leman, ed., *Lardil dictionary: A vocabulary of the language of the Lardil people, Mornington Island, Gulf of Carpentaria, Queensland: With English-Lardil finder list*, 12–56. Gununa, Queensland: Mornington Shire Council.

Hale, Kenneth L. 1998. On endangered languages and the importance of linguistic diversity. In Lenore A. Grenoble and Lindsay J. Whaley, eds., *Endangered languages: Language loss and community response*, 192–216. Cambridge: Cambridge University Press.

Halle, Morris. 1990. An approach to morphology. In Juli Carter, Rose-Marie Déchaine, Bill Philip, and Tim Sherer, eds., *Proceedings of NELS 20*, 150–184. Amherst: University of Massachusetts, Graduate Linguistic Student Association.

Halle, Morris. 1997. On stress and accent in Indo-European. *Language* 73, 275–313.

Halle, Morris, and Alec Marantz. 1994. Some key features of Distributed Morphology. In Andrew Carnie and Heidi Harley, eds., *Papers on phonology and morphology*, 275–288. MIT Working Papers in Linguistics 21. Cambridge, MA: MIT, MIT Working Papers in Linguistics.

Halle, Morris, and Ora Matushansky. 2006. The morphophonology of Russian adjectival inflection. *Linguistic Inquiry* 37, 351–404.

Harley, Heidi, and Elizabeth Ritter. 2002. Person and number in pronouns: A feature-geometric analysis. *Language* 78, 482–526.

Hartman, Jeremy. 2011. The semantic uniformity of traces: Evidence from ellipsis parallelism. *Linguistic Inquiry* 42, 367–388.

Harves, Stephanie. 2002. *Unaccusative syntax in Russian*. Doctoral dissertation, Princeton University. [https://files.nyu.edu/sah4/public/research/harves_diss.pdf]

Harves, Stephanie. 2003. Getting impersonal: Case, agreement, and distributive *po*-phrases in Russian. In Wayles Brown, Ji-Yung Kim, Barbara Partee, and Robert Rothstein, eds., *Formal Approaches to Slavic Linguistics 11: The Amherst meeting*, 235–254. Ann Arbor, MI: Slavica. [https://files.nyu.edu/sah4/public/research/Harves_FASL11 .pdf]

Haspelmath, Martin. 1993. *A grammar of Lezgian*. Berlin: Mouton de Gruyter.

Horvath, Julia. 2011. Oblique case assignment: Evidence from a case realization puzzle in Serbo-Croatian. Ms., University of Tel Aviv and MIT.

Ionin, Tania, and Ora Matushansky. 2004. A singular plural. In Benjamin Schmeiser, Vineeta Chand, Ann Kelleher, and Angelo Rodriguez, eds., *Proceedings of WCCFL 23*, 101–114. Somerville, MA: Cascadilla Press.

Ionin, Tania, and Ora Matushansky. 2006. The composition of complex cardinals. *Journal of Semantics* 23, 315–360. [http://jos.oxfordjournals.org/content/23/4/315 .abstract]

Irurtzun, Aritz, and Nerea Madariaga. 2010. On the syntax and semantics of DP internal scrambling in Russian. In Gerhild Zybatow, Philip Dudchuk, Serge Minor, and

Ekaterina Pshehotskaya, eds., *Formal studies in Slavic linguistics*, 287–302. Frankfurt am Main: Peter Lang. [http://www.ehu.es/nereamadariaga/Irurtzun&Madariaga%20Focus%20NP.pdf]

Isačenko, Alexander V. 1962. *Die russische Sprache der Gegenwart*. Halle: M. Niemeyer.

Isakadze, N. V. 1998. *Otraženie morfologii i referencial'noj semantiki imennoj gruppy v formal'nom sintaksise*. Doctoral dissertation, Moscow State University. [http://fccl .ksu.ru/issue002/autumn.99/isakadze.pdf]

Jackendoff, Ray. 1990. *Semantic structures*. Cambridge, MA: MIT Press.

Jakobson, Roman. 1984a. Beitrag zur allgemeinen Kasuslehre: Gesamtbedeutung der russischen Kasus. (Translated as: General meanings of the Russian cases) [1936]. In *Russian and Slavic grammar: Studies 1931–1981*, 105–134. Berlin: Mouton de Gruyter.

Jakobson, Roman. 1984b. Morfologičeskie nabljudenija nad slavjanskim skloneniem (sostav russkix padežnyx form). (Translated as: Morphological observations on Slavic declension (the structure of Russian case forms).) [1958]. In *Russian and Slavic grammar: Studies 1931–1981*, 106–133. Berlin: Mouton de Gruyter.

Johnson, Kyle. 2000. Few dogs eat Whiskas or cats Alpo. In Kiyomi Kusumoto and Elisabeth Villalta, eds., *University of Massachusetts occasional papers 23*, 47–60. Amherst: University of Massachusetts, Graduate Linguistic Student Association.

Kayne, Richard S. 1981. ECP extensions. *Linguistic Inquiry* 12, 93–133. [http://www .jstor.org/stable/4178206]

Kayne, Richard S. 2005. Some notes on comparative syntax: With special reference to English and French. In Richard S. Kayne, ed., *Movement and silence*, 277–333. Oxford: Oxford University Press.

Klokeid, Terry J. 1976. *Topics in Lardil grammar*. Doctoral dissertation, MIT. [http:// dspace.mit.edu/handle/1721.1/16398]

Kobiljanskij, B. V. 1953. Sintaksičnij zv"jazok kil'kisnyx čyslivnykiv *dva, try, čotyri* z imennykami (na materiali ukrains'koj i rosiys'koi mov). *Movosnavstvo (Naukovi zapysky Instytuta Movosnavstva AN USSR)* 12, 69–78.

Kondrashova, Natalia, and Radek Šimík. To appear. Quantificational properties of neg-wh items in Russian. In *Proceedings of NELS 40*. Amherst: University of Massachusetts, Graduate Linguistic Student Association. [http://www.sfb632.uni-potsdam .de/~simik/pdf/kondrashova-simik-neg-wh.pdf]

Koopman, Hilda. 2000. Prepositions, postpositions, circumpositions, and particles: The structure of Dutch PPs. In *The syntax of specifiers and heads: Collected essays of Hilda J. Koopman*, 204–260. London: Routledge.

Koopman, Hilda, and Anna Szabolcsi. 2000. *Verbal complexes*. Cambridge, MA: MIT Press.

Koroleva, M. 2005. Komnata dlja vnučki. *Rossijskaja Gazeta. Section: Nedelja.* 7 October 2005.

Kozyreva, T. G., and E. S. Khmelevskaja. 1982. *Sovremennyj russkij jazyk: Imja prilagatel'noe, imja čislitel'noe, mestoimenie*. Minsk: Vyšėjšaja Škola.

Kratzer, Angelika. 1995. Stage-level and individual-level predicates. In Gregory N. Carlson and Francis Jeffry Pelletier, eds., *The generic book*, 125–175. Chicago: University of Chicago Press.

Krys'ko, Vadim Borisovič. 1994. *Razvitie kategorii odushevlennosti v istorii russkogo iazyka*. Moscow: Licejum.

Lasnik, Howard, and Mamoru Saito. 1991. On the subject of infinitives. In Lisa M. Dobrin, Lynn Nichols, and Rosa M. Rodriguez, eds., *CLS 27*, 324–343. Chicago: University of Chicago, Chicago Linguistic Society.

Lechner, Winfried. 2006. An interpretive effect of head movement. In Mara Frascarelli, ed., *Phases of interpretation*, 45–70. Berlin: Mouton de Gruyter.

Lightner, Theodore. 1972. *Problems in the theory of phonology, vol. 1*. Edmonton, Alberta: Linguistic Research.

Lin, Vivian. 2000. Determiner sharing and the syntax of DPs. In Roger Billerey-Mosier and Brook Danielle Lillehaugen, eds., *Proceedings of the 19th West Coast Conference on Formal Linguistics*, 274–287. Somerville, MA: Cascadilla Press.

Mahajan, Anoop. 2000. Eliminating head movement. *GLOW Newsletter* 44, 44–45.

Marantz, Alec. 1997. No escape from syntax: Don't try morphological analysis in the privacy of your own lexicon. In Alexis Dimitriadis, Laura Siegel, Clarissa Surek-Clark, and Alex Williams, eds., *Proceedings of the 21st Annual Penn Linguistics Colloquium*, 201–225. Pennsylvania Working Papers in Linguistics 4.2. Philadelphia: University of Pennsylvania, Penn Linguistics Club.

Marelj, Marijana, and Ora Matushansky. 2010. Against overt predicators in Slavic. Talk delivered at GLOW Workshop on Slavic Syntax and Semantics. [Handout http://semantics.univ-paris1.fr/pdf/Against%20overt%20predicators%20in%20Slavic%20 2%203.pdf]

Matushansky, Ora. 2005. Going through a phase. In Martha McGinnis and Norvin Richards, eds., *Perspectives on phases*, 157–181. MIT Working Papers in Linguistics 49. Cambridge, MA: MIT, MIT Working Papers in Linguistics.

Matushansky, Ora. 2006. Head movement in linguistic theory. *Linguistic Inquiry* 37, 69–109.

McCawley, James D. 1993. Gapping with shared operators. In David A. Peterson, ed., *Proceedings of the 19th meeting of the Berkeley Linguistics Society*, 245–253. Berkeley: University of California, Berkeley Linguistics Society.

McCloskey, James. 1984. Raising, subcategorization and selection in modern Irish. *Natural Language and Linguistic Theory* 1, 441–485.

Mel'čuk, Igor A. 1980. Animacy in Russian cardinal numerals and adjectives as an inflectional category. *Language* 56, 797–811. [http://www.jstor.org/stable/413489]

Mel'čuk, Igor A. 1985. *Poverkhnostnyj sintaksis russkix čislovyx vyraženij*. Vienna: Gesellschaft zur Förderung Slawistischer Studien.

Mikaelian, Irina. 2013. Cardinal numeral constructions and the category of animacy in Russian. *Russian Linguistics* 37, 71–90.

Milner, Jean-Claude. 1978. *De la syntaxe à l'interprétation: Quantités, insultes, exclamations*. Paris: Seuil.

Moore, John, and David Perlmutter. 2000. What does it take to be a dative subject? *Natural Language and Linguistic Theory* 18, 373–416. [http://www.springerlink.com/content/g3m86468771um402/fulltext.pdf]

Neidle, Carol. 1988. *The role of case in Russian syntax*. Dordrecht: Kluwer.

Nesset, Tore. 2004. Case assignment in Russian temporal adverbials: An image schematic approach. *Glossos* 40, 1–52. [http://www.seelrc.org/glossos/issues/5/nesset.pdf]

Nevins, Andrew Ira, and John Frederick Bailyn. 2008. Russian genitive plurals are impostors. In Asaf Bachrach and Andrew Ira Nevins, eds., *Inflectional identity*, 237–270. Oxford: Oxford University Press. [http://www.ai.mit.edu/projects/dm/paradigms/bailyn-nevins.pdf]

Nikolaeva, Liudmila. 2007. Genitiv kačestva v russkom. Doctoral dissertation, Russian State University for the Humanities (RGGU).

Noonan, Máire. 2010. *À* to *zu*. In Guglielmo Cinque and Luigi Rizzi, eds., *Mapping spatial PPs: The cartography of syntactic structures, vol. 6*, 161–195. Oxford: Oxford University Press.

Obenauer, Hans-Georg. 1984. On the identification of empty categories. *The Linguistic Review* 4, 153–202.

Ouwayda, Sarah. To appear. Where plurality is: Agreement and DP structure. In *Proceedings of NELS 42*. Amherst: University of Massachusetts, Graduate Linguistic Student Association.

Penka, Doris. 2001. *Kein* muß kein Rätsel sein: Zur Semantic der negativen Indefinita im Deutschen. Doctoral dissertation, University of Tübingen.

Pereltsvaig, Asya. 2006. Small nominals. *Natural Language and Linguistic Theory* 24, 433–500.

Pereltsvaig, Asya. 2007a. *Copular sentences in Russian: A theory of intra-clausal relations*. Dordrecht: Springer.

Pereltsvaig, Asya. 2007b. The universality of DP—a view from Russian. *Studia Linguistica* 61, 59–94.

Pereltsvaig, Asya. 2010. As easy as two, three, four? In Wayles Browne, Adam Cooper, Alison Fisher, Esra Kesici, Nikola Predolac, and Draga Zec, eds., *Formal Approaches to Slavic Linguistics 18: The Cornell meeting*, 417–434. Ann Arbor, MI: Michigan Slavic Publications.

Pesetsky, David. 1982. *Paths and categories*. Doctoral dissertation, MIT. [http://dspace.mit.edu/handle/1721.1/15467]

Pesetsky, David, and Esther Torrego. 2001. T-to-C movement: Causes and consequences. In Michael Kenstowicz, ed., *Ken Hale: A life in language*, 355–426. Cambridge, MA: MIT Press.

Pesetsky, David, and Esther Torrego. 2007. The syntax of valuation and the interpretability of features. In Simin Karimi, Vida Samiian, and Wendy Wilkins, eds., *Phrasal and clausal architecture*, 262–294. Amsterdam: John Benjamins. [http://ling.auf.net/lingbuzz/000320]

Peškovskij, Aleksandr Matveevič. 1928. *Russkij sintaksis v naučnom osveščenii*. Moscow: Gosudarstvennoe učebno-pedagogičeskoe izdatel'stvo Ministerstva prosveščenija RSFSR.

Podobryaev, Alexander. 2010. How many splits in Russian: A view from LF. Paper delivered at Formal Approaches to Slavic Linguistics 19. College Park, MD.

Postal, Paul. 1974. *On raising*. Cambridge, MA: MIT Press.

Preminger, Omer. 2009. Breaking agreements: Distinguishing agreement and clitic doubling by their failures. *Linguistic Inquiry* 40, 619–666. [http://ling.auf.net/lingBuzz/000629]

Preminger, Omer. 2010. Failure to Agree is not a failure: Φ-agreement with post-verbal subjects in Hebrew. In Jeroen van Craenenbroeck and Johan Rooryck, eds., *Linguistic variation yearbook 9*, 241–278. Amsterdam: John Benjamins. [http://opreming.mysite.syr.edu/files/Preminger—Failure-to-Agree-is-Not-a-Failure—LIVY.pdf]

Preminger, Omer. 2011. Agreement as a fallible operation. Doctoral dissertation, MIT. [http://ling.auf.net/lingBuzz/001303]

Priestly, T. M. S. 1993. Slovene. In Bernard Comrie and Greville G. Corbett, eds., *The Slavonic languages*, 388–451. London: Routledge.

Rakhlin, Natalia. 2003. Genitive of quantification in Russian: What morphology can tell us about syntax. In Marjo van Koppen and Mark de Vos, eds., *Proceedings of CONSOLE XI*. Leiden, Holland: Student Organization of Linguistics in Europe. [http://www.hum2.leidenuniv.nl/pdf/lucl/sole/console11/console11-rakhlin.pdf]

Rappaport, Gilbert C. 2002. Numeral phrases in Russian: A Minimalist approach. *Journal of Slavic Linguistics* 10, 329–342.

Rappaport, Gilbert C. 2003a. Case syncretism, features, and the morphosyntax of Polish numeral phrases. In Piotr Bański and Adam Przepiorkowski, eds., *Generative linguistics in Poland 5*, 123–137. Warsaw: Academy of Sciences. [http://www.utexas.edu/courses/slavling/grapp/papers/glip5.pdf]

Rappaport, Gilbert C. 2003b. The grammatical role of animacy in a formal model of Slavic morphology. In Robert A. Maguire and Alan Timberlake, eds., *American contributions to the thirteenth International Congress of Slavists (Ljubljana, 2003)*. Vol. 1, *Linguistics*, 149–166. Bloomington, IN: Slavica.

Rappaport, Gilbert C. To appear. The Slavic noun phrase in comparative perspective. In Stephanie Harves and James Lavine, eds., *Comparative Slavic morphosyntax*. Bloomington, IN: Slavica. [http://www.utexas.edu/courses/slavling/grapp/papers/Slavnp.pdf]

Rezac, Milan. 2008. What will you have, DP or NP? In Daniel Harbour, David Adger, and Susana Béjar, eds., *Phi theory: Phi-features across modules and interfaces*, 83–129. Oxford: Oxford University Press.

Richards, Norvin. 2007. Lardil "case stacking" and the structural/inherent case distinction. Ms., MIT. [http://ling.auf.net/lingBuzz/000405]

Richards, Norvin. 2013. Lardil "case stacking" and the timing of case assignment. *Syntax* 16, 42–76. [DOI: 10.1111/j.1467-9612.2012.00169.x]

Riemsdijk, Henk C. van, and Riny Huybregts. 2001. Location and locality. In Marc van Oostendorp and Elena Anagnostopoulou, eds., *Progress in grammar: Articles at the 20th anniversary of the Comparison of Grammatical Models Group in Tilburg*, 1–23. Amsterdam: Meertens Instituut. [http://www.meertens.knaw.nl/books/progressingrammar/riemsdijk.pdf]

Riemsdijk, Henk C. van, and Riny Huybregts. 2006. Location and locality. In Simin Karimi, Vida Samiian, and Wendy K. Wilkins, eds., *Phrasal and clausal architecture: Syntactic derivation and interpretation*, 339–362. Amsterdam: John Benjamins.

Rosenbaum, Peter S. 1967. *The grammar of English predicate complement constructions*. Cambridge, MA: MIT Press.

Rouveret, Alain, and Jean-Roger Vergnaud. 1980. Specifying reference to the subject. *Linguistic Inquiry* 11, 97–202.

Schütze, Carson. 1997. Infl in child and adult language: Agreement, case and licensing. Doctoral dissertation, MIT. [http://www.linguistics.ucla.edu/people/cschutze/Dissert .pdf]

Schütze, Carson. 2001. On the nature of default case. *Syntax* 4, 205–238. [http:// onlinelibrary.wiley.com/doi/10.1111/1467-9612.00044/pdf]

Skoblikova, Elena Sergeevna. 1971. *Soglasovanie i upravlenie v russkom jazyke*. Moscow: Prosveščenie. Reprinted, Moscow: URSS (2005).

Solt, Stephanie. 2007. Two types of modified cardinals. Paper delivered at International Conference on Adjectives. Lille. [http://stl.recherche.univ-lille3.fr/colloques/adjectifs/ Abstracts/Solt.pdf]

Sportiche, Dominique. 2005. Division of labor between Merge and Move: Strict locality of selection and apparent reconstruction paradoxes. In Philippe Schlenker and Dominique Sportiche, eds., *Division of labor: The La Bretesche workshop*. [http://ling .auf.net/lingbuzz/000163]

Suprun, Adam Evgenievich. 1959. *O russkix čislitel'nyx*. Frunze: Kirgiz State University.

Sussex, Roland. 1976. The numeral classifiers of Russian. *Russian Linguistics* 3, 145–155.

Švedova, Natalja Julyevna. 1970. *Grammatika sovremennogo russkogo jazyka*. Moscow: Nauka.

Testelets, Yakov. 2011. Case deficient elements and the Direct Case Condition in Russian. Ms., Russian State University for the Humanities (RGGU), Moscow.

Timberlake, Alan. 2004. *A reference grammar of Russian*. Cambridge: Cambridge University Press.

Toops, Gary H. 2008. On the linguistic status of several obscure features of Upper Sorbian morphosyntax. *The Slavonic and East European Review* 86, 401–419. [http:// soar.wichita.edu/dspace/handle/10057/3513]

Travis, Lisa deMena. 1984. Parameters and effects of word order variation. Doctoral dissertation, MIT.

Travis, Lisa deMena. 1991. Parameters of phrase structure and verb-second phenomena. In Robert Freidin, ed., *Principles and parameters in comparative grammar*, 339–364. Cambridge, MA: MIT Press.

Vasmer, Max. 1986. *Ètimologičeskij slovar' russkogo jazyka*. Moscow: Progress. [Orig. 1950–1958; transl. O. N. Trubačëv.]. [http://vasmer.narod.ru/]

Vergnaud, Jean-Roger. 2006. Letter to Noam Chomsky and Howard Lasnik (1976). In Robert Freidin and Howard Lasnik, eds., *Syntax*, 21–34. London: Routledge.

Wechsler, Stephen, and Larisa Zlatić. 2001. Case realization and identity. *Lingua* 111, 539–560. [https://sites.google.com/site/wechslerpublications/publication-downloads/11WechslerZlatic2001-CaseRealization.pdf?attredirects=0]

Wiland, Bartosz. 2008. Circumstantial evidence for syntactic head movement. In Natasha Abner and Jason Bishop, eds., *Proceedings of WCCFL 27*, 440–448. Somerville, MA: Cascadilla Proceedings Project. [http://www.lingref.com/cpp/wccfl/27/paper1860.pdf]

Wiland, Bartosz. 2009. Aspects of order preservation in Polish and English. Doctoral dissertation, University of Poznań.

Xiang, Ming, Boris Harizanov, Maria Polinsky, and Ekaterina Kravtchenko. 2011. Processing morphological ambiguity: An experimental investigation of Russian numerical phrases. *Lingua* 121, 548–560. [http://www.sciencedirect.com/science/article/pii/S0024384110002573]

Yadroff, Michael. 1999. Formal properties of functional categories: The Minimalist syntax of Russian nominal and prepositional expressions. Doctoral dissertation, Indiana University.

Zaliznjak, Andrey Anatolyevich. 1967. *Russkoe imennoe slovoizmenenie*. Moscow: Nauka.

Zaliznjak, Andrey Anatolyevich. 1977. *Grammatičeskij slovar' russkogo jazyka: Slovoizmenenie*. Moscow: Russkij Jazyk.

Author Index

Subject Index

Linguistic Inquiry Monographs
Samuel Jay Keyser, general editor